TRADE, GLOBALIZATION AND SUSTAINABILITY

EMERGING ISSUES AND IMPACT ASSESSMENT

TRADE, GLOBALIZATION AND SUSTAINABILITY

EMERGING ISSUES AND IMPACT ASSESSMENT

BY

HARPER RYAN
ARIA LEE

KNOWLEDGE
BAKERS

KNOWLEDGE BAKERS

ISBN: 978-93-91502-83-6

Published by : **Knowledge Bakers**
Pune, India
Email: info@knowledgebakers.com

Digitally Printed at : **Replika Press Pvt. Ltd.**

PREFACE

Trade and globalization have transformed the world economy, connecting nations, cultures, and markets in unprecedented ways. While fostering economic growth, innovation, and cultural exchange, globalization has also raised concerns about its impact on the environment, society, and sustainable development. As we navigate the complexities of a globalized world, understanding the interplay between trade, globalization, and sustainability becomes essential for policymakers, businesses, academics, and civil society organizations seeking to address emerging challenges and promote inclusive and sustainable development. As we embark on this exploration of trade, globalization, and sustainability, we delve into a realm where economics, politics, and environmental science intersect, uncovering the principles, dilemmas, and opportunities that define the nexus between trade, globalization, and sustainability.

This book, titled "Trade, Globalization, and Sustainability: Emerging Issues and Impact Assessment," is crafted to provide a comprehensive resource for readers interested in understanding the complex interactions between trade, globalization, and sustainability and their implications for society, the economy, and the environment. Through collaboration with leading experts, policymakers, and researchers in the fields of trade, economics, sustainability, and environmental science, we aim to offer readers a multidimensional and insightful journey through the intricacies of these interconnected phenomena.

As editors of this volume, we have curated a collection of chapters that cover a wide range of topics in trade, globalization, and sustainability, including trade policy, global supply chains, environmental degradation, social inequality, labor standards, corporate responsibility, and impact assessment methodologies. Each chapter is designed to provide theoretical insights, empirical evidence, case studies, and policy recommendations to empower readers to understand and address the emerging issues at the intersection of trade, globalization, and sustainability.

Furthermore, this book seeks to highlight the importance of integrating sustainability considerations into trade and globalization policies and practices. By showcasing examples of how trade agreements, corporate strategies, and international cooperation mechanisms can promote sustainable development goals and address global challenges such as climate change, biodiversity loss, and social injustice, we aim to inspire readers to advocate for more inclusive, equitable, and environmentally responsible trade and globalization practices.

As we embark on this enlightening journey through the world of trade, globalization, and sustainability, we extend our gratitude to the contributors whose expertise and dedication have enriched this book. We hope that "Trade, Globalization, and Sustainability: Emerging Issues and Impact Assessment" serves as a valuable resource and source of inspiration for policymakers, practitioners, researchers, students, and advocates alike, empowering them to contribute to a more sustainable and resilient global economy and society.

Harper Ryan
Aria Lee

CONTENTS

CHAPTER 1

OUR GLOBALIZATION ERA AMONG SUCCESS, OBSTACLES AND DOUBTS

1. INTRODUCTION

1.1 The processes of globalization once historically defined

Contrary to the grammar definition of globalization according to the Oxford Dictionary ("the process by which business or other organizations develop international influence or start operating on an international scale"), to treat this topic we will take the first move from the well-known source Wikipedia, which more properly describes globalization as follows: "the process of interaction and integration among people, companies, and governments worldwide."

Once this working start could be accepted, we could rely on the following basic points, anyway to be analytically discussed:

- ☆ political interaction,
- ☆ stable economic relationships,
- ☆ cultural exchanges, included linguistic ones.

These processes are antique ones from the origins of the civilized word or so, dating back (just to synthetically exemplify) to Etruscan and Romans relationships, to Phoenician maritime trade, to inter-African economic exchanges, and—skipping some 1000 years due to common knowledge—to Marco Polo and Euro-Asian commercial traditions along the silk way, as well as to Euro-American ones after Colombo discovering the New Lands.

In every such cases, i) new political interactions immediately started, driving in rare cases to relationships on equality base but, more frequently, to the domination of a nation over other entities, this being the origin of colonial empires from Portugal onward; ii) stable and (rapidly) growing economic relationships on the basis either of mutual agreement or of widespread embezzlement, plunder, and sack, for example, Spain started a huge gold import from South America so as to give life to her cultural *siglo de oro* but, at the same time, to a dramatic inflation that started her decline; iii) cultural exchanges, in some cases consisting in the wrecking and crossing out of local cultures (this was the case of Australian natives after Captain Cook conquest in 1770), in other ones giving life to a confused, heteroclite merger of pre-existing and imported, of local and foreign, the so-called *enculturation*, and originating the reverse process, when, for example, the Greek culture deeply influenced the Roman one ("*Graecia capta ferum victorem cepit*").

In any case, not to say always, these processes brought about i) a dominant political authority, ii) its government, bureaucracies, laws, iii) its language, and iv) its money.

Every political domination, in fact, was of close lands or far ones, in every case accompanied by the following unifying processes, some of which are highly relevant both in those times and today, as still surviving ones:

- ☆ the unity of political and bureaucratic direction, the new official language included;
- ☆ the subdual to the same civil, penal, and fiscal laws (anyway with current local adjustments case by case);
- ☆ the direct connections between new motherlands and colonies from the point of view of transport routes, trade, and financial agreements or even impositions and monetary regimes (in some cases special ones, as the African French Franc).

This way, reflecting back to the political *equilibria* of the last five centuries broadly speaking, we propose to distinguish here, within the geographical processes of equalization of laws, money, and bureaucracy, the three following periods:

- the (sub)continental equalizations of a)1) the Roman Empire, especially at its climax, a)2) the Sacred Roman Empire of Charlemagne, a)3) the

Persian empire of prince Babur from Saudi Arabia to Iran to India, and a)4) the <Great China> of the Quing dynasty, especially under Kangxi, Yong-zen, Quian-long Emperors;

- the three early colonial empires of Holland, Portugal, and especially Spain;
- the intercontinental empires deriving from the second colonization conquests, giving life to French Empire and moreover to the British one, as at the end of the nineteenth-century Great Britain dominated 1/3 of world lands.

The above distinction offers us, as a matter of fact, the chance to quote a relevant, well-known interpretative category, the Gerschenkron model referred to the *sequence of sovereign powers*, showing step by step the decline of Spanish, Portuguese, and Dutch influence facing the larger strengths and world-wide ambitions of both England and France. Once the latter was confused by the troubles of the Revolution and its ups-and-downs follow-ups (as, after the loose of its American colonies, in addition it had to face three overturns of political regimes in just 26 years and one more some 50 years later), the room was left for the aggressive, goal-minded temper of Great Britain, while i) the Imperial Russia was isolated in her social and climate problems, ii) the Empire of Austria-Hungary secluded in Mid-Europe with no costal access but Trieste and too many different ethnic groups to be governed, and iii) to conclude with Germany and Italy still to be unified under, respectively, prince Bismarck and earl Cavour. These international dynamics can be summarized in Table 1.

Table 1. Rise and decline of states.

Relevant phases	Geopolitical orders
Mediterranean economy	Venetian domain and Maritime Republics
Northern and Western Europe	Northern European and Franco-German economies
Age of ocean navigation and discovery	Spain and Portugal
Dominance of Imperial China	Golden years of the Qing dynasty under Kangxi (1654–1722)
Replacement of maritime powers	Dominance of England until 1914
Scramble for Africa	European claims on African territories
US dominance	United States of America as dominant superpowers after 1944
Rise of Imperial Japan	Following the Meiji revolution (1852–1941) and then 1948–1990 (or 2000 according to others)
World expansion of China	The "Four Modernizations" after 1982
Source: authors' elaboration.	

At the same time, the abovementioned distinction, once generally interpreted, allows us to recall to memory one more well-known distinction, that is, the difference between i) land powers and ii) see powers. As a matter of fact as, Babur (and China) apart, in every remaining case the intercontinental domination was the fruit of naval strength and the military fleet to conquer, to preserve, and to secure commercial routes.

Moving first to the industrial revolution, thanks to its technical advances as well as the capitals accumulated by privateer war, England succeeded both in establishing a world domination and in impeding the existence in Europe of any leading country (or even alliance) able to jeopardize its supremacy, from Napoleon onward. Later, this natural behavior was theorized by relevant Anglo-Saxon admirals and scholars, Alfred T. Mahan, Halford J. Mackinder, Nicholas J. Spykman, among others. The supremacy we remember here declined anyway in favor of the USA, after the World War II (1941), Bretton Woods (1944), the atomic bombs on Hiroshima and Nagasaki (1945), the Marshall Plan (1948). This way, the supremacy of the pound sterling disappeared in favor of the US dollar, and similarly for the rest, beginning by the India independency (1949).

Not so curiously anyway—that's why we recall this theory here as globalization is regarded—in both cases these maritime superpowers realized (or tried, and the USA still try) the following realities: i) a unique country dominating the world, ii) a country isolated by the sea (or Oceans) but ready to intervene by the army in other countries or even continents, iii) under such political principles as *free market*, *monetary (and financial) supremacy*, *maritime strength*.

This rough overview of well-known century-old dynamics teaches us anyway some peculiar hints, judged relevant here with reference to the topic under discussion as in so many cases still surviving today. These suggestions respectively regarding the role of legal systems and its special regulations, the role of the (imposed) monetary regime, are still to create new currency (and financial) areas, the not-so-peaceful rotation of sovereign powers, a political struggle, which can be interpreted as the oligopoly competition, frequently leading to wars in their different forms.

1.2 The process of globalization and its technological drivers

The historical dynamics are so poorly recalled here in memory because of common knowledge, brought about, along centuries and decades, a dramatic increase of international exchanges of economic goods, financial and monetary resources, capital and investments, knowledge, cultures, and ideas. At the same time, they generated the parallel increase of international trade, this happening with the Industrial Revolution of England and the further ones (Table 2), from the United States of America to Belgium, and to France (once she overcame the troubles of the revolution) and to the following ones of Germany, Italy, and other countries.

Table 2. The three "industrial revolutions."

Features	The first	The second	The third
Year	1750 and following	1870 and following	1970 and following
Energy	Coal	Electricity, petroleum	Alternative energies
Production outcomes	Iron	Steel, chemistry	Informatics
Innovation	Steam engine	Internal combustion engine	Finance services and communications
Basic sectors	Textile industry	Mechanical industry	Financial and High-tech sectors
Source: authors' elaboration.			

In particular, the Congress of Wien marked the beginning of a long period of peace for Europe—a century—till the World War I, with the French-German war of 1870–71 being there an *entre-act* of nearly no relevance.

A century of peace meant, in addition, a century of technological progress (Table 3), this fuelling production, exchanges, communications, in such a way and in hurry we find it difficult to understand, and only comparable to the present Web revolution.

Table 3. The main inventions 1827–1939.

Invention	Year	Invention	Year
Battery	1800	Tyre	1887
Typewriter	1829	Diesel engine	1892
Dynamo	1831	Radioactivity	1901
Refrigerator	1834	Airplane	1903
Telegraph	1837	Cellophane	1908
Phone	1864–76	Penicillin	1928
Dynamite	1867	Television	1929
Phonograph	1877	Helicopter	1930
Internal combustion car	1885	Jet plane	1939
Source: authors' elaboration.			

The technical progress obviously influenced also public and private bureaucracies, work organization, labor relationships, these elements being constituting a relevant (and under-esteemed) factor in accompanying or even guiding the globalization process. On one side, new investments and the search for working (labor) resources oriented in fact internal and international immigrations; moreover, they contributed—in colonial Empires—to international investments, which, on their turn, further contributed to the globalization itself. On the other side, the new organizational techniques (e.g., Frederick W. Taylor) allowed to increase productivity, productions, salaries, profits, this fuelling once more offer, demand, and investments. Taylor's suggestions had been practically anticipated and largely applied in Krupp factories before 1910, and were later utilized for large-scale consumer goods by Henry Ford from 1923 onward.

Technological advances of those days fuelled since then inter-continental integration, giving life to larger international communications, higher import-export, more trade agreements, and widespread international investments (Gualino, a tycoon ruler of Italian finance end-nineteenth-early twentieth centuries largely invested in St. Petersburg, unfortunately before 1917, Pirelli & Co. vertically integrated acquiring rubber plantations in Malaysia). All the same, on a larger scale, is happening in today world, especially after 1948 (Marshall Plan), 1976 (China's Four Modernizations), 1991 (crumbling away of Soviet Russia), WTO, and WEB revolution.

With regard to the Four Modernizations, their purpose was to make China one great economic power, and the results are evident if we consider the evolution of the national shares of world production from 2000 to 2018 (Table 4).

Table 4. National percentage share of world production 2000–2018.

Nation	2000	2007	2009	2014	2018
China	8.2	15.4	21.5	32.8	28.4
USA	24.8	17.4	15.1	14.1	16.6
Japan	15.8	8.9	8.5	6.2	7.2
Germany	6.6	7.5	6.5	5.3	5.8
Italy	4.1	4.5	3.9	2.5	2.3
France	4	3.9	3.6	2.5	1.9
South Korea	3.1	3.9	3.6	3.7	3.3
India	1.8	2.7	2.9	n.d.	3
Brazil	2	2.6	2.7	n.d.	n.d.
Great Britain	3.5	3	2.3	n.d.	1.8
Source: authors' elaboration.					

1.3 Trade liberalization as a driver for globalization after the World War II

A further driver that oriented the globalization process after the World War II was trade openness [1], to which a set of factors contributed, such as [2]:

- ☆ the 1947 General Agreement on Tariffs and Trade (GATT) and the liberalization of international trade;
- ☆ the end of the Bretton Woods agreements (1971) and the resumption of international capital mobility;
- ☆ the development of new information and communications technologies (ICT) and the reduction or cancelation of distances, almost at no cost;
- ☆ the growing role of foreign direct investment (FDI) [3], which in the 1990s mobilized large amounts of capital, mainly from Europe and North America.

The above factors, together with others specifically referable to the individual geographical areas, led to a significant reduction in post-war trade barriers among the major industrialized countries, as well as a notable increase in capital movements [4].

In this regard, in addition to the GATT (1947), it is important to recall the creation of the European Common Market (1958 Treaty of Rome and 1968 customs union); the Canada US Free Trade Agreement (CUSFTA) of 1987; the North American Free Trade Agreement (NAFTA) of 1992; the ASEAN Free Trade Area (AFTA) Agreement of 1992; the establishment of the World Trade Organization (WTO) of 1995; and the General Agreement on Trade in Services (GATS) of 1995.

We mentioned above only a few among a number of trade agreements signed between the '40s and '90s of the last century. Also considering the 2000s, the increase in the number of regional trade agreements (RTAs) has been continuous and rapid (Figure 1).

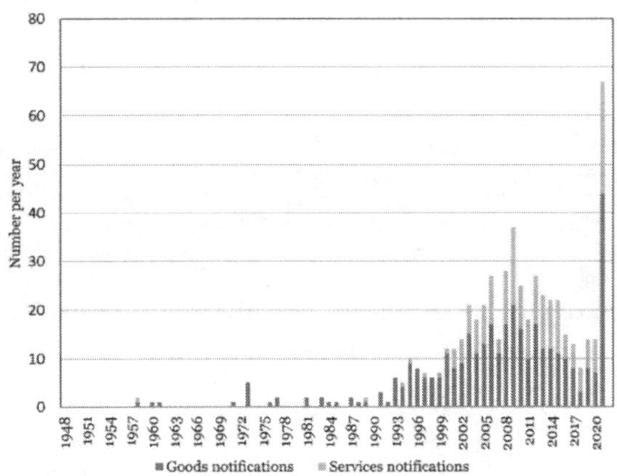

Figure 1. RTAs currently in force (by year of entry into force), 1948–2022. Source: WTO OMC, regional trade agreements database.

As pointed out by Urata [5], regional trade agreements (RTAs) remove trade barriers and significantly contribute to the quantitative and geographical expansion of international trade.

This expansion is clearly visible if we consider the evolution of the worldwide trade in the decade immediately following the signing of GATT (Table 5).

Table 5. Worldwide trade 1948–1990 (billion dollars).

	1948	1953	1963	1973	1983	1993	1999
Exports	58	83	157	578	1835	3639	5473
Imports	66	84	163	589	1880	3752	5729

Source: World Trade Organization, *International trade statistics* 2000.

In terms of percentage change, the growth of the world merchandise trade by selected region, which took place between 1990 and 1999, is presented in Table 6.

Table 6. Percentage change in the volume of world merchandise trade 1990–1999.

	World	North America	Latin America	European Union	Asia	Japan	Six East Asian traders
Exports	6.5	7.0	8.5	6.0	7.5	2.5	10.0
Imports	6.5	8.5	10.5	5.5	7.0	4.5	7.0

Source: World Trade Organization, *International trade statistics* 2000.

The positive effects of the trade agreements continued throughout the following decade, in which global trade growth remained sustained (Table 7). If we disregard the distributional consequences [6] and limit the analysis to the values exchanged, world exports continued to increase (Table 7).

Table 7. Global export value of trade in goods 2000–2008 (billion dollars).

	2000	2005	2006	2007	2008
Exports	6452	10,503	12,128	14,021	16,149

Source: https://www.statista.com/statistics/264682/worldwide-export-volume-in-the-trade-since-1950/ (accessed 6 May 2022).

The above data show the bivalence of globalization: On one hand, they reveal its positive effects on international trade; on the other hand, they show that the negative influences of crises of local origin (US), such as the 2008 financial One, spread with equal speed and magnitude, especially at the expense of weaker economies.

As a matter of fact, within economic integration—be it commercial or financial—the less-developed countries are generally dependent on the industrialized ones, with the consequent increase of their net indebtedness toward stronger economies. The subprime crisis caused profound effects and imbalances, to cast doubts on the real benefits of world integration in the absence of domestic growths [7].

In this latter respect, it is nevertheless relevant to consider that globalization, while not sufficient to reduce poverty on a large scale, anyway favors internal growth. According to Dreher [8], China was the country with the highest increase in the level of globalization from 1975 to 2000. Thanks to its increased integration with the rest of the world, the growth rate of its economy in 2000 was 2.33 percentage points higher than in 1975.

2. THE ROAD TO GLOBALIZATION AND THE NEW COMPETITIVE (DIS)EQUILIBRIA FOR FIRMS

2.1 Introduction

To treat the strategic problems of firms, it is maybe opportune to start by pointing out some basic differences between internationalization and globalization. The former was dominant from early twentieth century until the end of its '70ies, but the changes that occurred in the early '80ies produced a completely new type of phenomena, later on called—and not by a chance—*globalization.*

Undoubtedly, globalization changed the nature of competition as it was known before, when the number of international players was limited to firms possessing since decades, capital, knowledge, and the international culture to behave that way. Today, this number has gradually become larger and larger, a widespread one in every market and many (most?) industries of the world.

The main factors making globalization dominate since the '80s on are well-known ones: i) deregulation on one side and ii) the impact of new information and communication technology, the latter one maybe stronger than the former. Their interaction deeply changed the nature of markets and competition as well as the strategic behavior of companies, but also deeply influenced countries concerning international trade agreements, FDI, company law, that is, economic policies in one world [9, 10, 11, 12].

Deregulation enabled on one side companies to work more freely, especially as regards capital movements, international investments, mergers, and acquisitions, while information and communication technology on the other played a key role in accelerating global business transactions and deals, as they still do every day in a deeper way [13, 14].

Once transformed from international to global, competition showed largely new patterns of behavior, not to say completely renewed ones. Today, international players are in fact (and in particular they feel) more free than ever at every level (trade in goods and services, transfer of knowledge and technology, and FDI—Foreign direct investments and divestments), the latter ones representing one of the central nerves of restructuring global competition.

2.2 The strategic problems of firms within the new globalized era. Their strategic options and choices

This way, passing to firms' behavior within this largely new context, we could remember that, since its appearing, the enlarging of economic competition across continents was generally recognized by firms as a fruitful opportunity to grow. Anyway, this immediate feeling maybe undervalued at first sight its problems, challenges, and in some cases threats.

Globalization imposes in fact to big firms (but gradually also to mid-sized ones and to firms in general) a continuously growing confrontation with new competitors, a fierce one in some cases, which makes them suffer from the hardest competitive challenges.

As a result, companies must achieve a set of entirely new competences, among them i) to learn to make use of global resources (capitals, raw materials, finance, technology, labor, and others), ii) to make global their own products, and iii) to expand their own "local" competitiveness connecting it to new economic spaces, at the same time defending it from the challenges of other globalized firms.

In substance, companies must implement a global competitive strategy, expanding their markets but protecting at the same time their previous ones in case they can be now offended, as competitors too can individuate some competitive weakness to attack them, in spite of the fact they are (were?) locally dominated.

So, as all international firms are trying to put into action overlapping strategies, marketing techniques, products, services to customers, and tactics, this exacerbates the problem as such and drives to the need of implementing a *differentiation strategy*, in to contrast others firms' competitive actions, with the hopeful goal to enlarge market shares first, and profits as a consequence.

Does this mean that it is difficult for a company to become global in this era, and in case to remain such? This question brings with itself a former, fundamental one: How does a company compete in an unstable, difficult environment, establishing itself in this globalized world?

As a matter of fact, the term *differentiation strategy* covers a set of different strategic options to realize it, which could be synthesized as follows: i) cost competitiveness, ii) economies of scale, and iii) technological and marketing primacy [15, 16, 17, 18, 19, 20, 21, 22, 23].

2.2.1 Cost competitiveness

The pure cost competition, once intended as pure labor or raw material cost-reduction, is generally speaking a dated choice, a no-longer adopted one, due to the higher complexity of products, markets, and consumer needs at present. This problem is anyway a twofold one.

From the point of view of old industrialized countries, firms tend to transplant, that is, to relocate in other countries (and continents in case) paying today attention to geo-politics, closeness to final demand, transportation costs. Cost reduction keeps its own role for sure, but either related to the newest technologies together with highly skilled personnel (e.g., at present, Pirelli Tyres largely producing in Rumania) or connected only to segments of the whole production-cycle (e.g., Brooks Brothers in Tunisia, China, or even Indonesia).

From the point of view of the so-called third world countries, on their turn, also cost competitiveness entered into a wholly new dimension with globalization. As a matter of fact, thanks to the same globalization, those countries are not compelled to duplicate step by step for every technological stage from the beginning to present (as Rostov presumed) [24], as they can land on (very) recent technological stages—and in some cases on the more recent ones—this way being able to join modern technologies together with relatively lower salaries. The very example of this strategy is China, which rapidly joined this way the most advanced countries of the world and then overcame them in most cases, and the same China in recent years invested (and relocating) in South-East Asia, Africa, and elsewhere to be permitted to go on the same way.

2.2.2 Economies of scale

During the '60ies of the twentieth century, the microeconomic literature (and technical one as well) firmly suggested for firms the pursuing of "economies of scale," these ones mainly intended as large-scale plants and very large in case. The underpinnings of the proposal were rooted in the less proportional growth of some costs (energy, warehouse, internal connections, and surveillance) at the growing of the plant. With respect to pure theory as well as contrary to reality in its general terms, those merely technical suggestions ignored the true firms' dynamics: ups and downs of sales, plant and equipment rigidity, transportation costs, large or even impressive depreciation, and last but not the least, the local gathering of thousands of workers in a unique plant as a socioeconomic (and urbanistic) problem.

On this point, it is relevant to leave once for all the optimizing principles of early marginalists of the Walras-type, today unfortunately still widespread in most microeconomics text and since then constraining empirical phenomena into anti-realistic mechanical models.

Some of the most important scholars in the same field of economics are in fact teaching us since the last century how to cancel the very bases of those models:

- ☆ firms maximize /minimize/optimize in *subjective* a way, nor utilizing second-order Equations [25, 26, 27, 28, 29, 30];

- ☆ big firms are more interested in sales than profits, as in oligopolistic markets, it is more relevant to maintain and increase market shares, planning in case to make larger profits in future [31, 32];
- ☆ the whole firm-system is a complex organizational world, where special technicalities from the mathematical or statistical field must be applied uniquely to solve special technical problems of financial, productive, or commercial in nature.

After some decades of understandable oblivion due to the abovementioned imperfections and risks, also economies of scale took a quite different meaning with globalization. They are now no longer intended from the merely plant-scale and/or manufacturing point of view, but from the standpoint of general firms' costs. The new goals of firms pursuing "economies of scale" regard now, better than ever, the general optimization of i) purchasing, ii) R&D, iii) advertising costs, and iv) transportation ones as well.

The relevance today of such optimizations needs not to be underlined here, due to the increase of raw materials costs in the last decades on one side and the larger and larger amount of expenses implied by technological advances (high R&D within electronics, informatics, aerospace, military appliances), modern marketing techniques (especially for luxury goods, fashion, jewels, food, and drink), and farer and farer world deliveries in addition to energy and labor costs.

The convenience of large-scale plants tends to remain for industries—or branches of them—where firms actuate the fully integrated cycle (oil refining, basic chemicals, basic iron, and steel), where the same output in large amounts favors the scale of operations, this way taking profit from the efficiency of processes together with the reduction of logistic costs[1].

This whole system, anyway, provided market demand is growing or constant, or taking the minimum possible variance at least [33], not to accumulate unsold stocks or even being compelled to slow or stop the production; those risks concur in explaining the large success in the last 50 years of the so-called *mini-mills* as iron and steel is regarded.

In other industrial sectors producing industrial goods, the most important problem is given on the contrary by the ratio *cost per ton*, giving plants a limited space of action: In the cement industry, for example, this space is limited to 150–200 kilometers per plant—special cements apart—which explains the obliged multi-plant structure of its firms (e.g., *Cement Lafarge* (F) climbing some decades ago to more than 500 industrial plants).

This basic difference was underlined by the same Alfred Marshall, to be true only *at the end* of his life, clearly describing it as far as in 1919 [34]:

"The central task of the heavy steel industries is the handling of great volumes of homogeneous fluid steel, ready to be worked up into an infinite variety of products large and small. There is no other group of industries, in which the forces making for the increase of the business unit are promoted in like degree by the magnitude of the aggregate volume of the homogeneous fluid material which has to be produced.

The textile industries on the other hand offer the best instances of the coexistence of numerous establishments repeating one another; because the full technical economies of large scale production (...) can be obtained by an establishment of moderate size" (p. 218)[2].

In every case, as a conclusion, the problems for firms in general, and for plant in particular, are to individuate their critical dimension in relation to i) industry, ii) served markets and market segments, and iii) competitors.

2.2.3 Technological or marketing primacy, segmental dominance included

The above mentioned cross-world competition brought with itself large changes also as regards both technological and marketing primacies.

The need to be able today to sell all over the world emphasized the role i) of brands-innovation-advertising-distribution for high segments from electronics to information, to fashion and jewels, to cars to food-liqueurs-champagnes, and to armaments and weapons, ii) of brand and distribution for mid-level ones, and iii) of cost control and distribution for lower ones.

Innovation, performances, and in some cases uniqueness became relevant for luxury goods, price-quality relation for mid-quality ones, and price for lower ones.

In every case anyway, and much more frequently than before due to world communications and the WEB, brand recognizing became relevant for every market (the so-called world brands), but nevertheless also for specialized or "minor" segments, as these too got transformed from local-national to continental to world ones in some cases.

In addition, the larger economic resources expanded all over the world due to economic advances, to public and private debts, and to printing of money by States and privates (crypto-currencies), and increased both the quantity of demanded goods and the quest for quality by every group of consumers. Within industrialized countries, we face in fact today a large tendency to high tastes in every market and field, not to speak of such presences as advertising addicts /glamor influences/ till the reckless passions by the so-called fashion victims. These factors concur to explain the transition of many global firms to superior-upper segments of demand, and consequently to new product-portfolio strategies.

In addition, we must keep in mind that a further result is the fierce competition now in action, which implies a relevant increase of costs for every type of firm in particular as far as R&D, advertising, and distribution are concerned, the very local ones being the only ones excluded from these commitments.

A further problem is also represented by the insufficiency of i) mass production, ii) new design of products, and iii) price/quality levels conform to the new international standards, to guarantee the success of companies in the new era of globalization, or to make *per se* a company global. As a matter of fact, for most companies in the consumer goods industries, it is now necessary to be aware of getting new approaches regarding the following:

- ☆ trade, home consignments included,
- ☆ volume and more efficient distributing networks,
- ☆ transportation logistics,
- ☆ and, in particular for top segments,
- ☆ exclusive advertising,
- ☆ top class testimonials,
- ☆ loyalty ("club members" and more).

Testimonials (and moreover *influencers*) are equally important in mid-level segments, together with media advertising and, especially in the fashion industry, the opening of the so-called *sentinel point of sales* in cities where, right or wrong, be they San Francisco, Palm Beach, London, Paris, or others, and the individuation of styles /colors/fashion in general is forerunning the just subsequent mass tendencies.

Quite a different story, on their side, for producers of industrial goods, technical appliances and machinery in general, it is well known that in these fields the critical factors of success are quite different ones, mentioning here four of them just to remember the most important ones:

- ☆ technological advances,
- ☆ (experimented) special technical innovations together with their reliability,
- ☆ technical performance and performances /price ratio,
- ☆ fast technical assistance, at inter-continental level in case.

All the abovementioned factors contribute to explain the gigantic growth of M&A, mergers, and acquisition as a rapid tool to achieve, case by case, some special goals, or a multiple set of them as well [35]. According to the renewed company goals of today *multi-polar world*, divestment, acquisitions, and mergers in case can rapidly help in the following:

- ☆ growing to reach the so-called *critical dimension* with regard to productive capability, distributive structures, local presence in different countries/continents;
- ☆ focusing on a different productive and segmental equilibrium, which means completing the company *strategic map*, and selling low-growth activities, at the same time acquiring relevant capabilities and advantages from the point of view of brands, R&D, specialties, competences (as far as the former are concerned, the French case of LVMH is a seminal one in the field).

2.3 Globalization advantages and problems

Generally speaking, from the internal point of view we cannot forget that every competitive strategy by firms is closely related to system factors and the global organization as well, in particular concerning the following:

- ☆ the tension to goals by top managers (*key actors*) and their ability to communicate, motivate, and control;
- ☆ the nature and efficacy and efficiency of the internal structure,
- ☆ its organizational culture and behavior,
- ☆ the quality of coordination among strategic business units, together with the ability of the departments/units to join strategies choices and the global market [36].

Strategy is connected in fact to the quality and objectives of persons within every family, firm, institution, and country, but for firms in particular their growth is connected with the attempts of a particular group of human beings to do something [37][3].

As a matter of fact, some companies in the globalized world faced globalization in a courageous way with smart results later on, being able at the same time to take advantage of external opportunities and to adapt themselves to changes, and the dissemination of products and brands jointly being a goal and a result. They were able to anticipate competitors to nip at their heels taking into account i) the larger propensity of consumers to spend (not only in proportion to income but also recurring to debt), ii) the epochal changes in consumers' culture and values, and iii) the fast dynamics of consumers' tastes and needs, today from voluble to volatile ones.

As a result, these firms repositioned themselves, individuating innovative strategic directions to seize a competitive position among their (new) important competitors. They applied creative strategies in addition to previous ones—cooperation agreements, strategic alliances, M&A included—in line with their new *strategic location map* within the globalized world.

Some other firms, on their turn, followed the previous ones, which succeeded in engaging in global competition, anyway being at first generally undecided, topically dubious about the right road to be taken, organizationally conflicting about the timing and the dimension of new investments. This sum of problems caused in a large number of cases delays on one side and/or insufficient investments on the other hand, and both these problems being anyway partly repaired in some others cases by the wiser directions taken by looking at the experience of forerunners and eventually to their errors.

The remaining set of firms was reluctantly forced to renew themselves. Their delays were implied by a set of different, cooperating reasons, and among them, the following ones:

- ☆ their cultural approach to novelties, linked to locally minded markets, competitors, and strategies;
- ☆ their tendency to prioritize existing markets and product;
- ☆ the incertitude related to the amount of new commitments;
- ☆ their fear not to able to transition to globalization from the resource point of view as well as to orchestrate the new complexities implied by the horizon of activities [38, 39, 40, 41].

To these obstacles, it is easy to add the internal frictions among top managers, prominent shareholders, and also stakeholders in some cases, each of them reasoning maybe in terms of personal advantage rather than firm perspectives.

As a consequence, a set of companies suffered from serious problems represented by their inability to coordinate and harmonize on a large scale, and their previous practices are related to specialized segments, finance, technology, and their cultural and administrative skills as well.

All these problems negatively affected the strategic directions and current choices of these companies, which, still thinking in an improper way, tried somehow to imitate the most powerful and concentrated companies in the planet (USA, Europe, Japan) to get revitalized, anyhow with late, uncertain, or even unstable results, not to speak of cases when they took downward turns.

The main difference among them all lies in the fact that dominant companies, or prominent oligopolists, no longer really belong to one country only, while, in the perspective of globalization, other companies belonging to different countries still work on similar but partial strategies, which makes difficult even not impossible to obtain the same competitive advantages or defenses at least. The same difference between the two groups, which creates further dis-equilibria, acts on the ability of getting convenient means of production (capital, technology, human resources, raw materials, and others), where the first ones are largely favored by their timely entrance into globalization and globalized visions of the world. The only problem can be represented by conflicts and wars among countries: Globalization made easier the availability of those means for companies, making them more independent and profitable, but at the same time, it tends to make conflicts more intense or widespread ones.

3. OBSTACLES TO GLOBALIZATION, FROM DROP IN THE GROWTH TO POLITICAL ONES

3.1 Drops in the growth due to financial crises or emerging conflicts

After the protracted upward development of globalization described in Section 1, world trade fell sharply in 2009 (Table 8).

Table 8. Global export value of trade in goods 2008–2009 (billion dollars).

	2008	2009
Exports	16,149	12,556
Source: https://www.statista.com/statistics/264682/worldwide-export-volume-in-the-trade-since-1950/ (accessed 6 May 2022).		

Figures represented in Table 8 clearly show the drop in both growth and hopes caused by the bankrupt of both Fannie Mae and Freddie Mac.

The global financial crisis of 2008 was followed by an extremely fluctuating and sometimes stagnant trend in international trade (Figure 2).

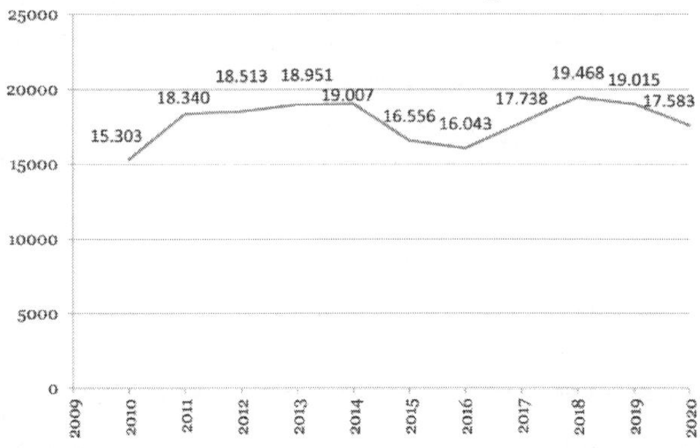

Figure 2. Global export value of trade in goods 2010–2020 (billion dollars). Source: Authors' elaboration based on data from https://www.statista.com/statistics/264682/worldwide-export-volume-in-the-trade-since-1950/ (accessed 6 may 2022).

In these sudden (or gradually postponed) storms, both businessmen and politicians ask themselves *what's around the corner*, while the latter ones—in short or mid-terms, also due to different visions of the world (*Veltanschauung*), competences, and vested interests—succeed in finding some solutions in near every case, normally damaging State budget by the increase of expenses to be "solved" by increasing debt or printing currency (or both).

The problem referred here is a well-known one, whose most important consequences are connected to i) the spatial extension and ii) the time span of the crisis.

While the latter can be traced back to the above mentioned political "solution," the former one is strictly connected to such factors as follows:

☆ the monetary dimensions of the crisis,

☆ its (in)direct influences on further either financial or banking crises,

☆ the psychological shocks it can produce,

☆ the degree of integration between the interested country and the world financial system.

Factors 1–3 are self-explaining ones, and in a sense the fourth too, about which we limit here to recall i) the dramatic effects of *Black Friday* on the world economy, ii) the large but not-so-dramatic effects of Freddie Mac & Co. in 2009, and iii) the effects of crises in some Latin America countries, repeated ones but regularly absorbed up to now.

Two more notations seem anyway of some interest here:

☆ the *timing* of diffusion of the crisis, as in today running economy its widespread is a nearly immediate on, while the Wall Street crisis of 1929 took on the contrary one year at least to propagate itself in Europe, due to the same time reason, the lesser speed of international trade (the financial one included) in those old days of near one century ago;

☆ the same *globalization* which we are treating here since pages, as the world integration of trade, finance, investments, and so on can widespread more than ever the effects of crises, of large ones in particular (not to mention here the high presence in the world portfolios of US$ bonds and shares together with debts of other countries they too denominated in US$).

Financial crises are anyway not alone in causing (heavy) disturbances to world economy, and globalization in particular. One more category storms includes all the more or less important mismatches occurring along years in different continents, *sudden overturning of regimes, revolutions, famines, vars.*

To recall here only the most dramatic of them, we could rapidly mention the French Revolution (1789), the crumbling down of the Chinese Empire (1911), the Soviet Revolution in Russia (1917), the pulling out of the Shah in Imperial Persia (1979), not to mentions the so many local military rebellions in Africa, South America, and elsewhere.

Mention apart is deserved, to better clear our topic, by the World War I, originated by apparently silly causes (the assassination of an Austrian Archiduke), but as a matter of fact signing the dramatic end of the unbelievable more than 40 years of expansion and growth of the Western World which on due course since the Franco-German War of 1871.

Treating these two kinds of problems, scholars turn by turn qualify these disturbances as *unexpected/ unimaginable/unpredictable* and so on. In parallel, they resume the old double couple of environmental "challenges and threats" for firms must strategically answer coping with their own "strengths and weaknesses." Be it of this kind, or even a more sophisticated one by the help of econometric models, this interpretation can be radically criticized on the bases of the systematic approach to the problem, suggested by a seminal contribution of 1933 by Ragnar Frisch (Nobel Prize in Economics 1969) [42].

This approach, which gave origin to a set a studies in particular in non-Anglo-Saxon world [43, 44][4], distinguishes two basic kinds of forces operating within economic dynamics, moving it currently or by exception, in regular v. erratica a way.

So, squeezing some thousands of pages in a few lines, we could describe Frisch interpretation as such the following:

- ☆ economic systems are composed by inner variables and choices as well as by external permanent ones, the former due to the actions of economic agents, and the latter represented by demography, politics, technology, competition, money&banking, and so on, which favor/ obstacle/orientate economic choices (*propagation variables*);
- ☆ this fusion of individual choices and permanent external influences might be *all of a sudden* changed /ruined/or even destroyed by external unforeseen *shocks*, which deeply changes the equilibria of the system (*impulse variables*).

Obvious to mention among most important impulse variables as the last 100 years are concerned, the World War I and II, the Sino-Japanese war of 1931 ff., the Italian war against Ethiopia 1934–1935 and—after some 20 years of peace 1944 (Bretton Woods) to Vietnam war (1964 ff.)—the set on international wars and disturbances, in addition to abovementioned ones, also the two *oil crisis* (1973 and 1980), the crumbling away of the Berlin Wall, and the disintegration of U.R.S.S. (1991) to give space at the end to the series of further wars in Iraki, Serbia, Lybia, and elsewhere.

Generally speaking, the political, sociocultural, economic, and industrial consequences of those impulse variables are well known ones to the reader, with general overturning—in worst cases—of boundaries, population distribution, public finance, industrial equilibria, but, at the same time, a fast development of technology, and so many advantages for the winner, if any. One more feature anyway to be mentioned—physical and financial destructions apart—is the common and general increase of prices, industrial, and consumer ones, which change the equlibria of families, firms, and in case the State in some cases in a dramatic way.

Propagation variables, each of them normally working with better or worse an equilibrium, are on their turn differently shocked by the aforementioned impulses, anyway under an immediate disorder under the pressure of the impulse ones. We conclude this flash leaving on one side the analysis of the consequences once more to the reader, and on the other listing the most important propagation variables:

- ☆ natural propagation forces:
  - demography,
  - psychologies,
  - technology;
- ☆ political propagation forces:
  - institutions,
  - international relations,
  - money, banking, and finance;
- ☆ half-endogenous propagation forces:
  - type and size of firms,
  - competition structures,
  - distribution of income and wealth (according to Pareto theories) [43].

3.2 The political side: Ideological oppositions, contrasting goals, government constraints

Cross-border acquisitions and all the more foreign direct investments are normally hailed by growing firms to sustain their expansion either within their own continent or in further ones as well. And we cannot deny that, decades ago, these activities were often conducted in the search of low-cost raw materials and labor in Latin America, South-East Asia, and mainly Africa. As we all know, this implied in not so few cases also workers' and environment exploitation, that convenient branching out being accepted by 3rd World countries with mixed sentiments just to favour their own economic development. The situation concurred this way to increase the differences between big industrial countries on one side, mid-sized half-industrialized ones on the other hand, and developing countries to conclude.

Along years, the so-to-say mismatching implied by these attitudes of foreign companies (ranking top down from US, Great Britain, France, and others shouting "profits profits!") drew public attention to the political, social, and cultural realms affected by their actions and behavior. This way, in hosting nations, some backlashes against globalization were registered within the civil society and by governments as well inducing in some cases a growing unwillingness to progress in multinational cooperation, better in multilateral co-operations of such a way. In worst cases, not only NGO-Non Governmental Organizations reacted to reputed exploitments, but a whole theory was developed—*Race to bottom*—lamenting, be that entirely true or not that globalization vas disrupting local economies, destroying previous national cultures, diminishing basic human rights in general workers' in particular, and threatening the preservation of the natural environment till degradation in case.

The last critics overvalued real cases of that kind as they had their roots in the anarchist-*green* mentality, and generally spoke against the so-called capitalism as the dirty imagine of free-market economy; in addition, they more properly referred, in case, to situations belonging to the twentieth century. After the Uruguay Round within GATT (1986–1993) and Doha development agenda (ended 2005), and as well, concerns had reduced and—the literature says—largely, even not totally dissipated. As a result, companies are now looking not for exploitation if any, but paying attention to the following characteristics of the host's country:

- ☆ stability of institutions,
- ☆ of infrastructures,
- ☆ of property rights, especially the foreign investors' ones.

Anyway, the calculus of costs and benefits has to be attentively weighted for both companies and host countries.

Companies gained only putative advantages, or even benefits shorter than expectations, putting into action egoistic behaviors, (un)voluntarily tending either to exploit or to make "easy money," taking advantage from their bargaining power irrespective of fairness, workers' /population/environment rights, in addition to the host-country interest in general. They must not only obey to these comprehensive ethical principles, but in addition to pay attention to the following technical factors:

- ☆ navigate the different legal systems of every foreign country (in particular as commercial and tax laws are regarded, tax payment included);
- ☆ to respect different labor laws granting protection to workers' rights;

- get adequately accustomed to different new cultures, which have to be also considered full of language/behavior/marketing/advertising teachings.

On the side of host countries, on their turn, they too must pay attention to a number of factors, including or even mixing advantages and risks. General and special advantages can be resumed as follows:

- of foreign trade, increase of occupation, developing of sub-contractors and sub-suppliers new firms, and growth of internal demand also due to the *multiplier effect*,
- from cultural and technological transfers, including modern management practices and advanced labor skills.

Some critical questions stay anyway in the background, as they need a (preferably a previous or a step-by-step) solution:

- general attitude toward foreign participation to their economic system, together with the conditions to welcome it, tariffs cutting included;
- degree, timing, and extent of liberalization of their own economy,
- putting into action of measures apt to expand their degree of participation in the world economy, through conditions at the same time consistent with i) country political independency defense, ii) human and workers' rights enforcement, and iii) environment protection safeguard.

4. CONCLUSIONS, OR GLOBAL INTEGRATION VS. LOCAL RESPONSIVENESS

Since first steps, globalization produced some contradictions between companies on the one hand and the governments of host countries on the other hand as regards the difference between wished and effective results. Many countries and companies fronted in fact difficulties in facing globalization at first, especially as objectives, trade, competition, and employment were concerned, and this lack of understanding increased in the first period; the gap between State regulation and company strategies, they both maybe undervaluing the burdens of the same globalization.

In terms of objectives, while State policies aimed to raise the standard of living, companies were looking to increase their market shares in order to grow, also due to a critical feature they understood, which could be summarized saying for most industries "grow to survive," not to be secluded in small or even local markets nor, at worst, to fail. This way companies were compelled to think in two ways, adopting a twofold competitive strategy, a two-dimensional one: i) the local dimension to be able to compete locally, with both traditional competitors and new ones from other countries, and ii) the transnational dimension to compete all over the continent or world with global(ized) firms.

This way expanding companies joined a new strategy to their previous ones, entering in local markets both to sell and to make FDI in the field of production, so gaining footholds in the global market. In relation to the deepness of those investments, strategies between local responsiveness and global integration began to take shape (Export strategy, Standardization strategy, Multi-domestic strategy, and Transnational strategy).

With globalization, also competition gradually became a global one, changing in nature as well as in ways and means. States soon or later adopted the goal of raising new standards of economic efficiency for the country as whole, and companies on their turn had to raise their own efficacy and efficiency up to the level of the *representative multinational firm*. This positively changed them, while modernizing indirect effects were widespread on countries' reputation as well as citizens' income, savings and demand, and culture. In general, it can be said that, as the two main characters—States and companies—focused on the new world standards, and the original gap between them was gradually reduced.

Originally, local governments concentrated themselves slowly, and in some cases so-to-say insensitively on globalization, to realize later on, especially in the last 20 years or so that it was relevant to enter into bilateral/multilateral trade negotiations in order to be active a part in the world development agenda, or at least to be able to protect i) local environment, ii) citizens' and workers' rights, and iii) the equality of conditions. Local regulations increased their span and deepness, as host' countries tended to set regulatory standards and restrictive policies for the implementation of international agreements and strategic cooperation, to reduce as much as possible the negative impact of globalization. In addition, also global regulations greatly increased their impact, especially in favor of States (or national governments) having limited contractual powers.

Once most countries found that there is no escape from globalization *while it lasts*, this new awareness led them to work to balance global integration and local responsiveness by hosted firms, making large adjustments at the macroeconomic and juridical level and, generally, favoring every kind of activity today "strategic" to promote companies but at the same time their own national interests.

REFERENCES

1. Lane PR, Milesi-Ferretti GM. The drivers of financial globalization. American Economic Review. 2008;98:327-332. DOI: 10.1257/aer.98.2.327
2. Crafts N, Venables AJ. Globalization in History: A Geographical Perspective. In: Bordo MD, Taylor AM, Williamson JG, editors. Globalization in Historical Perspective. Chicago: University of Chicago Press; 2003. pp. 323-370

3. Nunnenkamp P. Determinants of FDI in developing countries: Has globalization changed the rules of the game? Kiel Working Paper. 2002;1122:1-44

4. Harris RG. Globalization, trade, and income. The Canadian Journal of Economics/Revue Canadienne d'Economique. 1993;26:755-776

5. Urata S. Globalization and the growth in free trade agreements. Asia Pacific Review. 2002;9:20-32. DOI: 10.1080/13439000220141569

6. Stiglitz JE. The overselling of globalization. Business Economics. 2017;52:129-137. DOI: 10.1057/s11369-017-0047-z

7. Rodrik D, Subramanian A. Why did financial globalization disappoint? IMF Staff Papers. 2009;56:112-138

8. Dreher A. Does globalization affect growth? Evidence from a new index of globalization. Applied Economics. 2006;38:1091-1110. DOI: 10.1080/00036840500392078

9. Conversi D. Between the hammer of globalization and the anvil of nationalism: Is Europe's complex diversity under threat? Ethnicities. 2014;14:25-49. DOI: 10.1177/1468796813487727

10. Dunning JH, editor. Governments, Globalization, and International Business. Oxford: Oxford University Press; 1997

11. Haufler V. A Public Role for the Private Sector: Industry Self-Regulation in a Global Economy. Washington, D.C.: Carnegie Endowment; 2013

12. Loxley J. Interdependence, Disequilibrium and Growth: Reflections on the Political Economy of North-South Relations at the Turn of the Century. London: Palgrave Macmillan Limited; 2016

13. Doz Y, Santos J, Williamson P. From Global to Metanational: How Companies Win in the Knowledge Economy. Boston: Harvard Business School Press; 2001

14. Golding P. Forthcoming features: Information and communications technologies and the sociology of the future. Sociology. 2000;34:165-184. DOI: 10.1177/S0038038500000110

15. Brown P. The globalisation of positional competition? Sociology. 2000;34:633-653. DOI: 10.1177/S0038038500000390

16. Fleisher CS, Bensoussan BE. Business and Competitive Analysis: Effective Application of New and Classic Methods. Upper Saddle River, New Jersey: Pearson Education; 2015

17. Lim JS. Global integration or local responsiveness?: Multinational corporations' public relations strategies and cases. In: Golan GJ, Johnson TJ, Wanta W, editors.

International Media Communication in a Global Age. New York: Routledge; 2009. pp. 299-319

18. Luo Y, Tung RL. International expansion of emerging market enterprises: A springboard perspective. Journal of International Business Studies. 2007;38:481-498. DOI: 10.1057/palgrave.jibs.8400275
19. Romelaer P, Beddi H. Strategy and structure in international multi-business groups: Looking beyond global integration—Local responsiveness. International Studies of Management & Organization. 2015;45:359-378. DOI: 10.1080/00208825.2015.1006040
20. Roth K, Morrison AJ. An empirical analysis of the integration-responsiveness framework in global industries. Journal of International Business Studies. 1990;21:541-564. DOI: 10.1057/palgrave.jibs.8490341
21. Teney C, Lacewell OP, De Wilde P. Winners and losers of globalization in Europe: Attitudes and ideologies. European Political Science Review. 2014;6:575-595. DOI: 10.1017/S1755773913000246
22. Voelpel SC, Leibold M, Tekie EB. The wheel of business model reinvention: How to reshape your business model to leapfrog competitors. Journal of Change Management. 2004;4:259-276. DOI: 10.1080/1469701042000212669
23. Zoo C. Beyond the Core: Expand your Market without Abandoning your Roots. Boston: Harvard Business School; 2004
24. Rostow WW. The Process of Economic Growth. New York: Norton; 1952
25. Machlup F. Marginal analysis and empirical research. The American Economic Review. 1946;36:519-554
26. Baumol WJ. Economic Theory and Operational Analysis. 4th ed. Englewood Cliffs, New Jersey: Prentice Hall; 1977
27. Baumol WJ, Quandt RE. Rules of thumb and optimally imperfect decisions. The American Economic Review. 1964;54:23-46
28. Georgescu-Roegen N. Analytical Economics: Issues and Problems, Cambridge. U.S.A.: Harvard University Press; 1966
29. Kaldor N. The irrelevance of equilibrium economics. The Economic Journal. 1972;82:1237-1255
30. Demsetz H. The Economics of the Business Firm. Seven Critical Comments. Cambridge: Cambridge University Press; 1995
31. Baumol WJ. On the theory of oligopoly. Economica. 1958;25:187-198

32. Baumol WJ. The theory of the expansion of the firm. The American Economic Review. 1962;52:1078-1087

33. Kaldor N. later Baron Kaldor of NewnhamMarket imperfection and excess capacity. Economica. 1935;2:33-50

34. Marshall A. Industry and Trade. London: Macmillan; 1919. pp. 218-219

35. Doz YL, Hamel G. Alliance Advantage: The Art of Creating Value through Partnering. Boston: Harvard Business Press; 1998

36. CA. La strategia aziendale. Milano: Giuffré; 1984

37. Penrose E. The Theory of the Growth of the Firm. New York: John Wiley and Sons; 1959

38. Axinn CN, Matthyssens P. Limits of internationalization theories in an unlimited world. International Marketing Review. 2002;19:436-449. DOI: 10.1108/02651330210445275

39. Brecher J, Costello T, Smith B. Globalization from below: The Power of Solidarity. Cambridge, Mass: South End Press; 2000

40. James H, James H. The End of Globalization: Lessons from the Great Depression. Cambridge: Harvard University Press; 2009

41. Streeten P. Globalization: Threat or salvation? In: Bhalla AS, editor. Globalization, Growth and Marginalization. London: Palgrave Macmillan; 1998. pp. 13-47. DOI: 10.1007/978-1-349-26675-3_2

42. Frisch R. Propagation problems and impulse problems in dynamic economics. In: Economic Essays in Honor of Gustav Cassel. London: Frank Cass & Co. Ltd.; 1933. pp. 171-205

43. Demaria G. Trattato di Logica Economica. Vol. III. Padova: Cedam; 1974

44. Perroux F. Unités actives et Mathematiques nouvelles. Paris: Dunod; 1976

CHAPTER 2

SUSTAINABILITY AND EXCELLENCE: PILLARS FOR BUSINESS SURVIVAL

1. INTRODUCTION

Nowadays, the quality of products, including services, appears the mandatory criterion that must be taken into account by companies all over the world. In order to better organize their activities, the companies design, implement, and then review business management systems.

ISO standards offer a framework that covers different areas and give companies support regarding the design and implementation of the management systems.

To ensure a certain degree of quality in all the levels and areas, the company designs and sets in place the quality management system (QMS), in accordance with the fundamentals presented in ISO 9000 [1] and the requirements given by ISO 9001 [2].

In the last decade, to have a quality system implemented in the company appears not enough to identify all the problems and solve them or to face in a reliable way the changing environment. After some time, the systems need to be evaluated in order to identify their performance. For realizing the self-assessment of the QMS, the standard ISO 9004 [3] comes in handy.

To offer a broader alternative to ISO 9004, the excellence models have been developed and reviewed to facilitate benchmarking and maturity level assessment in terms of performance [4, 5, 6, 7, 8]. One of the most developed and used Excellence Model is the European Foundation for Quality Management (EFQM) Excellence Model [4, 5, 6].

As the industry evolved taking into account the quality of products, processes, machines, and systems, another problem appeared that it is not covered in total by the tools used in order to analyze the performance (ISO 9004 [3] and Excellence Models [4, 5, 6]). The excellence models were the starting point of finding solutions for a sustainable development of companies.

In order to achieve sustainable development for a company, the three pillars, namely society (social responsibility), economic growth, and the environment protection, must be taken into account [9].

In 2010, ISO drafted and published the standard ISO 26000 [10] that offer companies' guidelines considering two of the three pillars (society and environment). Its purpose is to harmonize the social behavior of enterprises worldwide [10, 11, 12].

An important item in sustainability is the establishing of key performance indicators and the manner in which they have to report them. To have guidelines for reporting, the Stitching Global Reporting Initiative (GRI) and ISO have developed a framework for companies presented in GRI1 Foundation [13]. The next three standards cover the part of general disclosures [14], materials [15], and economic performances [16]. The first four GRI standards are applied in all fields.

Nowadays, searching companies' websites, more and more companies exhibit their strategy in terms of customer focus and sustainability. Moreover, sustainability strategies are promoted to increase customer loyalty showing the approaches for sustainable development so as to harmonize stakeholders into more sensitive balance between environment – human – development – policies.

2. FUNDAMENTAL CONCEPTS FOR SUSTAINED ORGANIZATIONAL SURVIVAL

One may analyze the structure of ISO standards concerning quality management, i.e., the fundamentals (ISO 9000 [1]), the requirements (ISO 9001 [2]), and the guidance for sustained success that may be considered an assessment framework and tool for the QMS maturity (ISO 9004 [3]). The QMS principles are accompanied by possible actions, these actions being translated into requirements in ISO 9001 [2]. This means that one may not focus unbalanced on one or another component of the system, the whole, as a system, appears relevant, and all aspects should be considered irrespective of the priority order selected by the organization to address the fundamental through approaches.

Once implemented, the organization may step into the next level of performance, applying the self-assessment regularly in order to define improvement plans and act accordingly. In this context, ISO 9004 offers a maturity assessment tool [3] finalized with a radar diagram for better evidence of the areas with more potential or emergency need for improvement. Such a radar, together with the detailed maturity assessment, may be used by the management team (top and middle) as a prioritizing tool for the decision-making process.

If organizations maintain into the improvement cycle according to ISO 9001 requirements, certainly certain benefits may be reported on long term, but, in order to proactive reply to the global changes, ISO standards appear too basic to release organizational adaptability and people real engagement. The management team has the option to support improvement projects, even beyond the ISO requirements, such as motivating people through different mechanisms to balance professional to private life or involvement in community responsibility projects. On short term, the tangible effect may be more satisfaction and engagement of people.

Based on the experience of different contexts, in function of the organizational capability, a significant step ahead may be embracing extended fundamentals of an excellence model, such as EFQM [3, 4] or other similar business models. Table 1 presents in comparison the fundamentals showing the consistency in progression of these principles.

Table 1. Comparison of fundamentals.

Quality management principles [2]	Fundamental concepts EFQM model [4]	Fundamental concepts updated EFQM model [5]
	Achieving Balanced Results	Sustaining Outstanding Results
Customer focus	Adding Value for Customers	Adding Value for Customers
Leadership	Leading with Vision, Inspiration & Integrity	Leading with Vision, Inspiration & Integrity
Engagement of people	Succeeding through People	Succeeding through the Talent of People
Process approach	Managing by Processes	Managing with Agility
Improvement	Nurturing Creativity & Innovation	Harnessing Creativity & Innovation
Evidence-based decision making		
Relationship management	Building Partnerships	Developing Organizational Capability
	Taking Responsibility for a Sustainable Future	Creating a Sustainable Future

Once a sound management system set in place and a deep commitment of the management team for these fundamentals, the use of the excellence model framework is naturally adopted. Even more complex, more evidence-based, more refined, and in-depth interconnected, the excellence model offers to the management team the framework for assessment on a broader and more discrete perspective in order to define action plans for improvement. Similarly, but more complex, all fundamentals should be considered, each of them having corresponding criteria and subcriteria, and the same maturing assessment is proceeded, revealing finally the areas for improvement.

The difference, but the added value of the excellence model, lies into the more refined evidence research for more organizational cells and layers, seen in the progression of PDCA (Approach – Deployment – Assessment & Refinement) of the assessment so as to identify, prioritize, and implement sustainable approaches.

Table 2. Assessment grid for enablers.

Type of evidences	Attributes	Rating %
Lack of indicators Lack of procedures Interfaces undefined	No evidence or anecdotal/Unable to demonstrate	0%
Indicators set in place, but no monitoring and connection with the approaches Improvement plan drafted Procedures for critical issues Interfaces coordination in an unformal way	Partial Conformity/ Some evidence/ Limited ability to demonstrate	25%
Improvement plan documented and monitored Procedures/processes set in place, documented and functional Functional interfaces Rare or minor disruptive processes/few or minor non-conformities Monitored indicators as decision-making process threshold/framework	Effective/ Evidence/Able to demonstrate	50%
Regular improvement of the documented processes Regular update of procedures for better and more fluent functioning Interfaces regular monitoring together with process stakeholders	Efficient/Clear evidence/ Fully able to demonstrate	75%
Innovative approaches set in place Practices reference for benchmarking at global level Anticipation of needs and their evolution Committed and motivated actors Continuous learning from the implemented approaches to explore perceived opportunities	Excellent/ Comprehensive evidence/ Recognized as global role model	100%

Even if the model changed the role from an assessment tool [4, 5] to a framework for defining the direction so as to cocreate together with others a sustainable ecosystem [6], in order to understand the capabilities and to address the necessary changes, the assessment grid (Table 2) is given for connecting to evidences while analyzing the reality, in order to define priorities for present and future.

3. FRAMEWORK FOR DIAGNOSTIC OF MATURITY LEVEL OF ORGANIZATIONAL PERFORMANCE

Disruptive processes appear nevertheless in any environments and nowadays change, balance, technology, transformation may not be avoided; moreover, after a long period of stop-and-start, with direction research in the pandemic time, which revealed clearly that previous solutions should be reviewed and soundly transformed, a diagnostic of the entity's reality is needed.

The RADAR tool has been developed on the basis of the Deming cycle (Plan-Do-Check-Act) but adding the organization's reason of existence in the ecosystem, measured through the results composed by perceptions and outcomes/outputs/indicators, all of these benchmarked versus targets.

Table 3. Radar assessment framework for enablers.

	Element	Detail	Rating %	Organization reality
R	**Results**	What are the results aimed to achieve as follows the Strategy	Search evidence and assess	Strengths and Areas for improvement
A	Plan and develop sound and integrated **Approach**es to deliver the Results in a sustainable way	Sound—considering relevant stakeholders needs build Approaches with real rationale and define processes to support them	Search evidence and assess	Strengths and Areas for improvement
		Integrated—considering the Strategy to achieve the Results, build and connect the Approaches in a sustainable and synergetic structure		
D	**Deploy** the Approaches in a structured way to support sustainable achievements	Implemented—approaches are implemented in relevant areas with time refinement based on the stakeholders present and future needs	Search evidence and assess	Strengths and Areas for improvement
		Systematic—approaches are operational and enable resilience and agility; Approaches are planned and executed soundly		

	Element	Detail	Rating %	Organization reality
A	**Assess** the deployed Approaches analyzing the achieved Results and the ongoing learning experiences	Measurement—regular measurements of approaches effectiveness & efficiency, regular measurements of effectiveness & efficiency of carried out deployments, appropriate measurements selected and regularly monitored	Search evidence and assess	Strengths and Areas for improvement
R	**Refine** the deployed Approaches analyzing the achieved Results and the ongoing learning experiences considering the changing environment	Learning and creativity—internal and external good practices/practices to avoid and improvement opportunities are internalized and valorized, approaches and deployments are updated with creativity		
		Improvement and innovation—outputs from measurements and learning and creativity are feeding evaluation, prioritization, planning and implementation of improvements and innovations		
Summary per Enabler subcriterion			Consolidated rating	Strengths and Areas for improvement

Table 4. Assessment framework for results.

Element	Detail	Rating %	Organization reality
Relevance and usability Results should be comprehensive, reliable, accurate and consistent with the strategy	Scope and relevance—performance seen as strategy to fulfill relevant stakeholders needs and expectations is demonstrated by coherent and sustained key results (KPI)	Search evidence in relevant areas and assess	Strengths and Areas for improvement
	Integrity—results are accurate and reliable and ensure confidence		
	Segmentation—to reveal meaningful insights		

Element	Detail	Rating %	Organization reality
Performance positive trends and sustained good performance, comparisons are favorable against best in segment or class, cause-effect relationships allow confidence into sustainable performance	Trends—sustained positive performance at least 3 years	Search evidence in relevant areas and assess	Strengths and Areas for improvement
	Targets—are set and are consistently achieved, in line with the strategic objectives		
	Comparisons—external comparisons are made and these are favorable, in line with the strategic objectives		
	Confidence—the performance level will be sustained as enablers—results relationship is conditioned		
Summary per Result subcriterion		Consolidated rating	Strengths and Areas for improvement

The assessment/diagnostic tool allows the management team to analyze in depth the working style in order to manage more effective and efficient, but to enable the strategy and plans definition in clear priority and consistent follow-up. The starting point is the results aimed to achieve, once determined, approaches are set in place to deliver these results, approaches become operational through deployments, and their effectiveness, efficiency, and sustainability are assessed and refined. The assessment framework is detailed in Table 3 for enablers and Table 4 for results.

For a better understanding of how the day-to-day activity of the organization should be framed into the excellence assessment, some guidance is presented in Table 5. Current tools, developments, and ways of working may be associated to enablers, but the management thinking design should always be mirrored by the results (perceptions and outcomes) assessment and their evolution understanding, compared with targets and adequately/dynamically benchmarked. The cause-effect relation helps in understanding the "why" behind the organization's approach, the "how" to deploy the approaches, and the achievements as a result, in practice the consequence of all these actions.

Table 5. Guidance for enablers.

Enabler	Subcriterion	Possible approach	Possible deployment
Leadership	Leaders develop the Mission, Vision, Values, Ethics and act as models	Define the core business purpose for a sustainable future and consequently the Values and Ethics	Vision, Mission, Values are developed and integrated into the Strategy and communicated regularly to all stakeholders
		Define and review leaders code of conduct/ agreed behaviors to explicit the leaders role model	Enable assessment, review, improvement of individual performance, mainly those of leaders
		360° Appraisal - evaluate leaders performance based on feedback from all levels of interaction top, down and lateral	Deploy a sound process of assessment of the individual performance so as to build a culture of trust and ethics
	Leaders define, monitor, review and improve the management system and the performance	Set strategic measures to monitor performance in line with the stakeholders needs and expectations, such as Balanced Scorecard	Management team assess progression against targets set so as to achieve the strategic goals; composite indicators are regularly analyzed as part of the decision process
		Management board meetings for regular review and refinement in line with the business	Strategic objectives are cascaded into the reporting processes (financial, operational a.s.o)
	Leaders engage with external stakeholders	Regular contact of senior management with key customers, partners and community representatives	Define business to business strategic level and review it regularly in line with the strategic goals
		Reporting and public communication, such as Sustainability report (UN Global Compact)	The reports content, format and circulation concern business key financial, environmental and societal progression, in line with international initiatives committed for, if the case
	Leaders reinforce the culture of excellence with organization's people	Define the culture of excellence by adopting a business model in line with an excellence model, such as EFQM	Consider excellence as a reference in the planning processes; leaders actively involve people in improvements
	Leaders ensure that the organization is flexible and manage changes effectively	Annual Board Meeting—the Board communicate the plans and gain support/commitment for their implementation	The management team agrees the strategic plans and gain support, if the case, from shareholders
		Annual kick-off event—leaders communicate the overall strategy and the annual objectives	Leaders adopt organization's objectives and cascade them to individual ones in their teams

Enabler	Subcriterion	Possible approach	Possible deployment
Strategy	Strategy is based on understanding both stakeholders' needs and expectations and external environment	Understanding developments, opportunities, threats on the desired and current market	Relate market analysis with strategic partners, knowledge management and research and development, connect with academics a.s.o.
		Understand any updates concerning legal and regulatory compliance	Legal and operational teams should cooperate to identify and implement the regulatory and compliance framework and correspondent actions to set in place
	Strategy is based on deeply understanding internal performance and capabilities	Perform an in-depth self-assessment conducted internally or externally; Cross check with control systems results	Perform an in-depth self-assessment to identify priorities for the action plans; Consider objectively the organization's capabilities
	Strategy and policies are developed and updated to ensure sustainability	SWOT analysis may reveal internal and external perspectives (Strengths, Weaknesses, Opportunities and Threats)	Balance internal and external perspectives in strategy, policies and strategic plans
	Strategy and policies are communicated and deployed/documented	Strategy mapping—strategy is geographically segmented and aligned with stakeholders' expectations	Strategy maps may be communication tools and review tools for the management team to check performance and update the objectives, plans, processes
		Cascade objectives—align personal and teams' objectives although the organization with the strategic ones	Start from top level and progressively break down through functional streamlines and individuals; Connect individual objectives with internal communication and the appraisal process
People	People plans are aligned with the organization strategy	People engagement rather than people satisfaction	Enable people's contribution to their full capacity to the organization goals; Link people engagement to customer loyalty and key results
		Recruiting process—attract, evaluate and select new and potential talented people	Promote mobility, link to remuneration and benefits policies, adapt to the level of people to be recruited, third part/external service may be used

Enabler	Subcriterion	Possible approach	Possible deployment
		Succession planning—identify potential successors for the key roles and prepare them adequately	Prepare business continuity planning on immediate and long-term perspective and review regularly the planning
	People's knowledge and skills are developed	Appraisal process—assess individual performance and behaviors against a set of agreed objectives, competences, attitudes	Align organization's overall objectives to people individual performance and objectives; Link to people survey and to performance related incentives (salary, bonus, promotion... penalty)
		Personal development and training—align individual needs to competences needed for the role as derived by the strategic objectives	HR strategy is aligned to people capabilities, organizational needs to fulfill the strategic goals and the appraisal process; Training plans are drafted and implemented, results of training are assessed and valorized
		Management development programs and/or people certification	Talent management plans set in place; Staff certification for roles needing it or for professionals in industry/sector setting the requirement, eventually on regular basis
	People are aligned, engaged and empowered	Process improvement teams—improvement as culture in a structural process	Privilege cross-functional teams; Involve (experts) facilitators or include training to guide the process
		5S—workplace and flows organization methodology	Empowering people to improve the workplace and the processes they are involved in; Facilitate processes' standardization
		Objectives' cascade—align individuals to strategic objectives	Connect to strategic planning process (ex-ante) and the appraisal process and people motivation policies objectively supported by people performance (ex-post)
	People communicate effectively throughout the organization	Internal communication—clear communication channels top, down, horizontal, inter-departments/units	Ensure a bilateral way of communication to support dialog and information transfer, based on needs of people and teams; Use surveys to assess the effectiveness

Enabler	Subcriterion	Possible approach	Possible deployment
		Electronic communication media	Encourage communication and networking through e-means (intranet, blogs, social networking a.s.o.), but maintain and valorize physical interaction, too
		Workers council	Develop a sustainable partnership with the workers' structures, if any
	People are recognized, rewarded and cared for	Rewards and benefits	Develop a flexible benefit package aligned to overall HR strategy
		Salary benchmarking	Screen the connection between people's motivation incentives and benefit package in the region, industry, sector etc. (external service may be used)
		Health and safety	Implement legal and regulatory compliance in term of occupational safety and health; Bonus as medical insurance, welfare, facilities for family
Partnership and resources	Partners and suppliers are managed for sustainable benefit	Suppliers' selection criteria	Suppliers' audits, assessment
		Establish, develop and manage relationship with partners	Partnership-related processes clearly defined, monitored and assessed; Partners' performance reported (impact on KPI) and related to Strategy
	Finances are managed to secure sustained success	Budgeting process, with data in compliance to legal regulation, stock exchange a.s.o.	Ensure budget are aligned to strategic objectives; Budget allocations are cascaded and aligned with processes and reviewed, correlated with the Results
		Procurement processes, lengths of supply chains	Responsible purchasing is a key for CSR strategy
	Buildings, equipment, materials and natural resources are managed in a sustainable way	Buildings' policy and facilities management to ensure a safe working environment with all necessary facilities for achieving the Strategy	Effective management of sites, locations, outsourced facilities Assess people satisfaction Report sustainability Review the policies
		Environmental management system Information security management system	Consider ISO certifications (ISO 14001, 27001 a.o.)

Enabler	Subcriterion	Possible approach	Possible deployment
	Technology is managed to support strategy	Possible IT outsourcing Internal digital transformation processes	IT maintenance, support, other services IT policies aligned to strategic goal People training and support
	Information and knowledge are managed to build operational capability	Knowledge management system Ensure data security, availability, integrity	Build a knowledge management system Capitalize the organizations' knowledge
Processes, Products and Services	Processes are designed and managed to optimize the value for stakeholders	Process approach and risk-based thinking	ISO 9001 implementation/certification
		Lean Six Sigma	DMAIC to understand performance dynamics and identify improvement options Monitor customer experience
	Products and services are developed to create value for customers	Research and development	Sustainability issues, production techniques, end life cycle monitored, recycling, buy-back, research on as-used components
		Focus groups to collect and generate new ideas, direct feedback	Involve customer in testing new products Collect regularly the Voice of Customer (VOC)
	Products and services are effectively promoted and marketed	Strategy of marketing / product launching, including target audience, value proposition, pricing, promotion	Clear definition of target audience; Use effective channels for reaching audience Assess the marketing campaign through the effective results
	Products and services are produced, delivered and managed	Supply chain management to ensure effective delivery of products and services to customer	Connect CSR into the supply chain management
	Customer relationships are managed and enhanced	Customer relationship management—a system set in place tracking contacts, accompanied details of expectations	Connect to product development, marketing-sales and performance indicators
		Customer centers	Sometimes outsourced Dependent on customer strategy adopted
		Customer surveys, the most common tool to collect customer experience	Frequency, segmentation, use of results to drive improvements and review of strategy

4. SUSTAINABILITY FRAMEWORK FOR COMPANIES

Considering the evolution of the industrial fields nowadays and the requirements stated by the standards and laws, companies have adopted more often the concept of sustainability. The sustainability development of a company is given by the three pillars of sustainability (see Figure 1): society (social responsibility), economic growth, and the environment protection. The three pillars are embedded within the company's management systems.

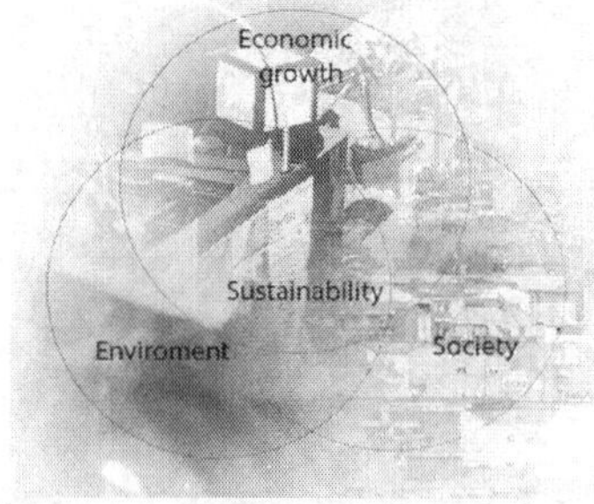

Figure 1. Sustainability pillars.

Since the first pillar of sustainability—economic growth—has been defined, this has appeared important for companies to remain in competition in their field of activity. In order to maintain a constant economic growth, companies define strategic objectives and continuously implement these objectives in all areas of improvement identified using several types of performance models. This pillar may relate to the first two enablers presented in Table 5: Leadership and Strategy.

Second and third pillars of sustainability development cover the other three enablers presented in Table 5: people, partnership and resources, and some parts of processes, products, and services.

The three pillars are, also, reflected in the Business Continuity Plan of companies, plan required by the legal norms in each country. Every company must consider and establish possible actions to keep under control the impact on the society and environment in any given situation.

In order to support companies and harmonize their social behavior, the International Organization for Standardization (ISO) has created the standard "*ISO 26000: 2010, Guidance on Social Responsibility*" [10].

The standard contains voluntary guidance, but it does not need a certification. Table 6 presents an example of steps that can be followed in order to implement the standard. Before implementing the ISO 26000, the most important step is to identify the stakeholders of the company and the impact they have on the social responsibility decisions that will be taken and implemented (see Figure 2).

Table 6. Implementation of the ISO 26000 standard.

	Steps	Possible actions
Plan	Identify the need benefits of implementing SR standard in the company	Establish the SR characteristics
		Identify the relationship between SR and sustainability
	Define the policy and the strategy	Identify stakeholders
		Identify and create a common ground between the values of the company and the SR values
		Analyze the SR principles
		Analyze and identify the needed areas for the company considering the seven core subjects of SR
DO	Integrate in the existing management system the SR requirements	Adopt the SR principles
		Establish the SR objectives
		Establish the KPI (key performance indicators) for SR
		State the action plan
	Implement the possible actions	Establish the way of reporting the KPI
		Raise awareness in the company
		Integrate the action plan in the company systems
	Communicate and set the reporting means for all the stakeholders	Identify the most effective way of communication
		Engage the stakeholders taking into account their impact on the company decisions regarding SR
		Analyze the SR influence
		Report the KPI established
Check	Evaluate	Monitor the SR performance
		Analyze the data obtained
Act	Improve	Identify possible action in order to improve the SR performance Track the improvements impact

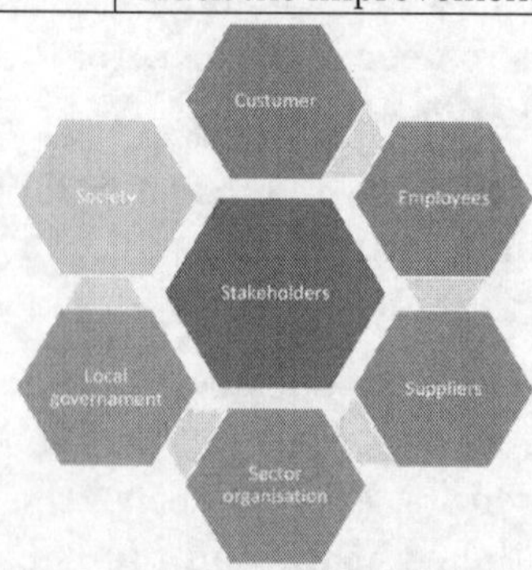

Figure 2. Stakeholders.

Table 7. The core subjects from ISO 26000 [10].

Core subject	Relevant areas of interest	Stakeholders
Organizational Governance	The application of the SR principles ensures an elevated level of organizational governance	The organization leaders Employers
	A joint effort is needed, considering the size of the Organization, to achieve the desired results associated with SR.	
	The most effective mechanism to implement is to maintain the motivation of the stakeholders and to proper develop of the principles of Social Responsibility	
Human Rights	Establish transparent and effective complaint and redress mechanisms	The organization leaders Employers Customers Suppliers Society Local government
	"Equal rights for all employees and workers (such as gender equality) Strive for diversity in the employee group"	
	Freedom of opinion and expression	
	Contribution to economic, social and cultural rights	
	"No child labor and no forced labor Freedom of association or collective bargaining "	
Labor Practices	Contracts for employees with clear and correct mentions	The organization leaders Employers
	Equal and equitable opportunities for all employees	
	Contracts with clear and fair mentions to subcontractors, suppliers and partners	
	Protection of personal and private data of employees	
	Social protection for employees	
	Collaboration and openness to dialog with independent representatives representing the interests of employees	
	Continuous communication with local communities or other local stakeholders	
	Implementation of occupational medicine systems	
	Emergency assistance	
	Handling/Handling of Dangerous Equipment	
	Preventive Medical Investigations	
	Staff development and training plan	
	Training program for new employees	

Core subject	Relevant areas of interest	Stakeholders
Environment	Respecting and promoting the following principles: environmental responsibility cautious approach environmental risk management the polluter pays	The organization leaders Employers Customers Suppliers Society Local government
	Pollution prevention through management: emissions to air discharges into the water waste management use and disposal of toxic and dangerous chemicals other identifiable forms of pollution	
	Sustainable use of resources through the effective use of the following: basic raw materials electricity gas water	The organization leaders Employers Society
	Climate change mitigation through effective management of greenhouse gas emissions, Reducing vulnerability to floods	The organization leaders Society
	Valorization and protection of biodiversity	
	Valorization and Sustainable use of land and natural resources Restoration of ecosystems	
	Progress on ecological urban and rural development	
Fair Operating Practices	Clear rules regarding the accepted level of giving and receiving business gifts Respecting the local culture	The organization leaders Employers Costumers Suppliers
	Verification of certificates and declarations of origin	
	Establishing rules and boundaries regarding political lobbying	
	Similar level of information available to all providers and contractors	
	Contracts including clear terms and fair prices in relation to suppliers and	
	Honest pricing policy with suppliers	
	Implement appropriate vigilance mechanisms	
	Payment of fair compensation for intellectual and physical property rights	

Core subject	Relevant areas of interest	Stakeholders
Consumer Issues	Clear, honest and complete information about the products or services delivered and their impact.	The organization leaders Customers Employers
	Mechanisms for returning and withdrawing the product from the market.	
	Reliable, accurate, and verifiable information about the impact of products/services on the environment, society or economy	
	Adequate and relevant information on: product health and safety, possible negative impacts, maintenance, assembly or recycling.	
	Products that can be recycled or repaired and reused	
	Accessible and efficient customer complaint mechanism	
	Mechanisms for proper installation, use, repair, maintenance, return and recycling	
	Clear and fair guarantee and implementation mechanism	
	Mechanism for resolving disputes, resolving disputes, and mediating at a minimum cost to consumers	
	Transparent mechanism for obtaining, using, securing, and deleting personal data	
	The right of the customer/consumer to verify personal data	
	Protection policy for the provision of essential services to all consumers	
	Education and awareness program for customers/ consumers regarding the purchase conditions, comparison of key functions, impact of use, etc.	
Community involvement and development	Analysis of communities affected by core activities	The organization leaders Society
	Review of supporting the Millennium Development Goals or local development goals	
	Education and learning program for communities	
	Plan for respecting cultural traditions and protecting cultural heritage	
	Participation in local and national skills development programs, including apprenticeships	

Core subject	Relevant areas of interest	Stakeholders
	Plan for the direct creation of local jobs	
	Collaboration with universities or institutions in stimulating and providing technology at accessible local conditions	
	Providing fair opportunities for local suppliers and SMEs	
	Fair fiscal policy	
	Program to support communities with essential health care services, access to clean water, good sanitation	
	Activities to stimulate the improvement of the infrastructure for transport, water, electricity, communications, etc.	

The NEN Handbook "The implementation of SR – Best practices and tools for ISO 26000" offers a set of detailed free tools that can be used to implement the Social Responsibility (SR) in companies (see Table 6).

In order to implement the SR principles and objectives in the organization management, first of all, the relevant areas of interest correlated with the core subjects of ISO 26000 should be identified. In Table 7 are presented some relevant areas that can be important for different companies.

Companies that have implemented ISO 26000 and monitor sustainability should annually report the key performance indicators they set. In order to do that, they can use the reporting framework given by the GRI.

5. CONCLUSIONS AND PERSPECTIVES

Analyzing the common ground of the excellence models (EFQM) or sustainability, one may notice that for both approaches the companies must:

- ☆ Set objectives considering the fundamental concepts that the company has adopted and internalized in the company's culture
- ☆ Identify KPI for both and then ways and tools to monitor them
- ☆ Evaluate the performance on a regular basis
- ☆ Report the results
- ☆ Relaunch the cycle considering the performance and results versus the targets and comparing to the competitors when resetting the objectives.

Considering a company that adopted both excellence and sustainability concepts and codefined the company's values starting from these fundamentals, one may propose the structure of the company's management system looking similar to the Greek temple, as presented in Figure 3.

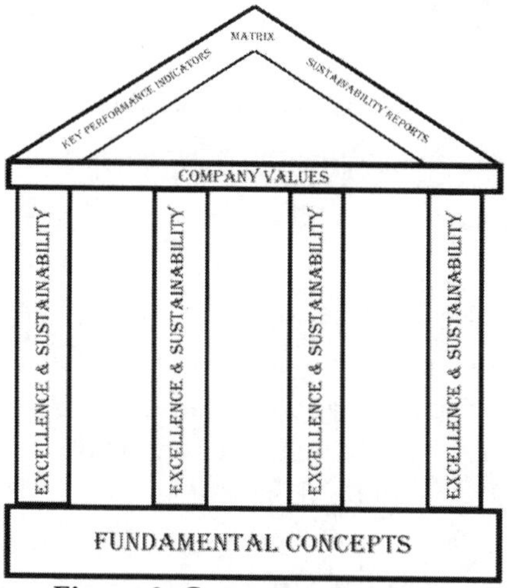

Figure 3. Company structure.

The foundation to build a surviving business may embed the fundamental concepts of excellence and sustainability, the pillars for maintaining the business in the global competition should arise from the two models, merging the enablers and the results of excellence with the criteria to assess sustainability, and finally, the company assesses and reports regularly the KPI and the other metrics in order to better comply with the values, to differentiate among competitors, and to better serve the stakeholders.

REFERENCES

1. Quality management systems — Fundamentals and vocabulary (ISO 9000:2018)
2. Quality management systems – Requirements (ISO 9001:2015)
3. Quality management – Quality of an organization – Guidance to achieve sustained success (ISO 9004:2018)
4. EFQM Excellence Model. EFQM; 2010
5. EFQM Excellence Model. EFQM; 2013
6. The EFQM Model. EFQM; 2019 ISBN 978-90-5236-845-0
7. Quista J, Skalen P, Clegg SR. The power of quality models: The example of the SIQ model for performance excellence. Scand. J. Mgmt. 2007;23:445-462
8. Fukeya LN, Issac SS, Balasubramanian K, Jaykumar V. Service delivery quality improvement models: A review. Procedia-Social and Behavioral Sciences. 2014;144:343-359

9. Hermundsdottir F, Aspelund A. Sustainability innovations and firm competitiveness: A review. Journal of Cleaner Production. 2021;280(Part 1):124715. DOI: 10.1016/j.jclepro.2020.124715
10. Guidance on Social Responsibility (ISO 26000: 2010)
11. Obi D. An Introduction to Iso 26000 and Social Responsibility, BULLETIN No. 90/2014. Geneva, Switzerland: International Trade Centre; 2014
12. Stefanova M. ISO 26000:2010 – Guidance for process management of corporate social responsibility. In: Proceedings of the 10th Anniversary International Conference “Standardization and Related Activities – A Means of International and Balkan Collaboration”, Sozopol. Technical University - Sofia, Science Days, Sozopol-Bulgaria; 13-14 September; 2013
13. Foundation (GRI 1: 2021)
14. General Disclosures (GRI 2: 2021)
15. Material Topics (GRI 3: 2021)
16. Economic Performance (GRI 201: 2016)

CHAPTER 3

RETHINKING AN APPROACH FOR SUSTAINABLE GLOBALIZATION

1. INTRODUCTION

This chapter explores the relationship between globalization and sustainability and proposes an approach for sustainable globalization. There is an ongoing debate about the impacts of globalization on sustainability [1, 2] with arguments for both positive [3] and negative [4] impacts. An attempt is made in this chapter to advance this debate by proposing a framework for sustainable globalization. Interactions between globalization and sustainability are analyzed to tackle a complex question of whether globalization can be made sustainable.

The term sustainability is used here to refer to sustainable ecological systems that can be affected by factors such as resources consumption and pollution that impact biosphere functions [5]. The traditional three pillars [6] of sustainability, namely environmental, economic, and social pillars, are considered while also acknowledging that a primary core of sustainability is its concern for the well-being of the future generations [7]. Likewise, this chapter adopts the broad definition of globalization as a process that encompasses the causes, modalities, and consequences of transnational and transcultural integration of human and nonhuman activities [8]. Focus is given to economic and social components of globalization while also touching upon its political component.

Firstly, interaction between globalization and environment is examined by considering energy and resources consumption, greenhouse gases emission, and pollution (Section 2). Then, relationships of sustainability with the current green growth paradigm and alternative economic approaches are explored in the context of globalization (Section 3). Implication of globalization on social sustainability is then examined by taking into account the quality of life, urbanization, and social equality (Section 4). Based on the analyses of different interactions, existing knowledge gaps are discussed (Section 5). Then, an approach for sustainable globalization is proposed (Section 6), and finally, the conclusions are presented.

2. GLOBALIZATION AND THE ENVIRONMENT

There are several approaches to evaluate environmental sustainability. Environmental Performance Index has been used as a composite indicator to evaluate the state of sustainability of 180 countries by considering 11 issue categories [9]. These categories are air quality, sanitation and drinking water, heavy metals, waste management, biodiversity and habitat, ecosystem services, fisheries, climate change, pollution emission, water resources, and agriculture. Similarly, Environmental Performance Assessment Composite Index has been developed in [10] by combining three indices associated with natural resources, sustainable and efficient use of resources, and use of alternative resources. Likewise, six broad thematic categories—energy performance; waste management; air quality and pollution; water quality and pollution; land use, agriculture, and fisheries; and biodiversity, forests, and soils—have been proposed by [11] as indicators of environmental sustainability.

Ecological footprint is another common quantitative metric for measuring environmental sustainability. Basically, it is the amount of land, measured in global hectares, required to support a particular lifestyle [12]. Although the ecological footprint gives a valuable quantitative measure of environmental sustainability and enables comparisons of bio-capacities of different nations, it does not take technological change and underground resources into account [13]. Furthermore, it does not take land degradation into account [14].

Based on the adaptations from above mentioned studies, this chapter characterizes environmental sustainability in three broad categories of energy and resources consumption, greenhouse gases emission, and pollution to evaluate the interactions between globalization and environmental sustainability.

2.1 Energy and resources consumption

Globalization has a potential to cause both increase and decrease in energy and resources consumption. Globalization can increase the applications of improved technologies in low- and middle-income nations that lead to higher process and energy efficiencies, eventually reducing the energy and resources consumption. Contrastingly, globalization could also support economic growth that requires higher energy and resources consumption [15].

A popular measure of globalization is the KOF Globalization Index (KOFGI), which measures globalization along the economic, social, and political dimensions for different countries [16]. The 10 most globalized nations based on KOFGI [17] are all high-income nations in Europe that also have very high energy consumption per capita [18]. However, the material footprints of these nations are decreasing over time with the exception of Sweden and Denmark [19]. Material footprint is one of indicators of the United Nations Sustainable Development Goals and refers to the total amount of raw materials extracted to meet final consumption demands [20]. It may be noted here that the 10 most globalized nations have material footprints higher than the global average, and the majority of them have footprints higher than the European Union average [19]. It is also noteworthy that 50 most globalized nations [17] are primarily high-income nations with a few upper middle-income nations such as Malaysia and Thailand [21].

Energy consumption of top Asian economies has been found to increase with globalization [22]. It has been reported that the physical quantities of goods traded internationally only represent one-third of the actual natural resources that were used to produce these traded goods [23]. Therefore, it can be argued that globalization is currently increasing energy and resources consumption.

2.2 Greenhouse gases emission

Globalization, evaluated in terms of KOFGI, has been shown to increase greenhouse gases (GHG) emission in European Union [24] and Japan [25]. On the other hand, globalization has been found to reduce GHG emission in emerging economies such as Brazil, Russia, India, China, Mexico, Indonesia, and Turkey [26, 27] showing some evidence for Environmental Kuznets Curve (EKC) hypothesis. This hypothesis states that an inverted-U-shaped relationship exists between different pollutants and per capita income, i.e., environmental pressure increases up to a certain level as income goes up and then decreases. The KEC hypothesis is based on a notion that environmental quality deteriorates at the early stages of economic development and subsequently improves at the later stages [28]. The hypothesis is that as the economic development occurs at the expense of the environment, average income of the population increases. Once the average income is sufficiently high, a turning point is reached where people start to value and take care of their local environment. Technological solutions and energy efficiency enabled by the economic growth then allow for improvement of the local environment, since people can afford to take care of the environment.

2.3 Pollution

Impacts of globalization on local pollution other than GHG emission are presented here. International trade has been found to contribute to significant portion of total air pollution, which is negatively impacting human health [29, 30, 31]. It has recently been estimated that almost everyone on Earth is affected by air pollution [32]. Likewise, globalization may also be contributing toward land degradation. For instance, clearance of native vegetation and land degradation across much of Latin America and Asia has been linked to agricultural expansion and intensification at a commercial scale for export markets [23]. Likewise, there is also an indication that international trades facilitated by globalization are causing higher water pollution in emerging economies such as China [33].

In the context of emerging economies, there are studies showing support for, as well as against, the EKC hypothesis. For instance, support for EKC hypothesis where environmental quality first degraded due to globalization and then improved after the average income became sufficiently high was reported in several Chinese cities by [34]. Contrarily, continued environmental degradation in China was found by [35] despite the average income being sufficiently high, thereby showing evidence against the EKC hypothesis.

Plastic pollution may also be affected by globalization. For instance, China banned the import of plastic waste in 2017 to tackle its plastic pollution problem [36]. Although many high-income nations have agreed to place a strict limit on export of plastic waste to poorer nations, American exporters are still exporting plastic wastes to poor nations [37]. This can cause significant plastic pollution in poor nations that import plastic wastes.

3. GLOBALIZATION AND ECONOMY

This section analyzes the interaction between the existing green growth economic model and sustainability in the context of globalization. Alternatives to green growth economic models are also explored.

3.1 Green growth paradigm

The Organization for Economic Co-operation and Development (OECD) has a green growth strategy set in place since 2011 [38]. The OECD views green growth as an approach to foster economic growth and development while ensuring that natural assets continue to provide the resources and environmental services on which our well-being relies [38]. The United Nations has a similar concept of green economy, which is a low-carbon, resource-efficient, and socially inclusive economy. Growth in the green economy is driven by public and private investments based on the understanding that natural assets are critical economic assets [39]. An umbrella term "green growth" is adopted in this chapter to refer to any growth-based economic models.

Green growth assumes that economic growth can be decoupled from environmental pressures. In order to evaluate green growth, an approach to measure it has been proposed by comparing gross domestic product (GDP) with resources productivity [40]. Green growth is said to occur when percentage increase in resources productivity is higher than the percentage increase in GDP. For instance, if a country experiences a GDP growth of 2%, and its carbon productivity improves by 4%, the country displays green growth in the climate dimension [40]. Carbon productivity here is an example of resource productivity and is a measure of GHG emission reduction. Overall, green growth should reduce environmental pressure.

Economic components of globalization such as foreign direct investment and trade openness are promoted in OECD countries to accelerate green growth, and it has been found that these components help reduce GHG emission [41]. However, although the implementation of green growth has the tendency to reduce GHG emission [42], global GHG emission is expected to be record high as the world economy recovers from coronavirus [43]. For instance, both China and India surpassed their 2019 emission peaks in 2021. Chinese emission grew by 5.5% between 2019 and 2021, while Indian emission grew by 4.4% [43].

3.2 Alternative economic models

Critics of the green growth paradigm argue that empirical evidence on resource use and carbon emission does not support green growth theory [44]. It has been argued that there is no empirical evidence to suggest that absolute decoupling from resource use can be achieved on a global scale while continuing economic growth [44]. Consequently, alternatives to green growth have been explored. Degrowth and policies for social equity are examples of alternative to green growth [45].

Degrowth paradigm relies on a construct that continuous economic growth and ecological sustainability are incompatible. Therefore, it argues for reduced production and consumption. Likewise, policies for social equity (PSE) are based on a concept that inequality leads to environmental degradation. The PSE is actually a type of green growth with two added radical social policies, namely a job guarantee program and working time reduction [45]. Degrowth, on the other hand, contains the PSE but also argues for downscaling economy. While all the three economic models have their own advantages and disadvantages, simulations of green growth, PSE, and degrowth have shown degrowth model to be most effective in tackling environmental pressures [45].

4. GLOBALIZATION AND SOCIETY

This section explores the interaction between globalization and society in the context of social sustainability. Three aspects of society, namely quality of life, urbanization, and equality, are considered.

4.1 Quality of life

In low-income nations, life expectancy has been positively correlated with globalization [46]. Likewise, quality of life measured in terms of human development index has been found to increase with globalization in several Asian countries [47]. At global scale, aggregate positive effect from globalization-related trade has been reported while also acknowledging disproportionate distributional concerns. The disproportionate concern is that globalization-related trade can lead to unemployment, reduced wages, and slower decline in poverty in some geographical regions and commercial sectors [48].

The overall effect of globalization on high-income, as well as low-income, nations is reported to be improved quality of life. Positive impacts include harmonization of the labor market, development of digital society [49], and reduced macroeconomic volatility due to diversification of risks.

4.2 Urbanization

Urbanization is primarily happening in low- and middle-income countries due to economic growth and globalization [50]. Benefits of urbanization are increase in employment opportunities, abundance of unskilled labor, and expansion of industrial, residential, entertainment, and commercial areas. Urbanization and trade openness can also reduce income inequality [51, 52], particularly when coupled with high institutional quality and democracy. However, a study in Africa has found that urbanization alone may not significantly impact equality in the absence of democratic reforms and institutional quality [52]. Institutional quality here refers to corruption control, law and order, and sound bureaucracy. On the flip side, disadvantages of urbanization include increased crime and land use change [50]. Farmland loss, ecological degradation, and decrease in biodiversity are some of the negative consequences of urbanization [53].

4.3 Equality

The relationship between equality and globalization is very complex. Generally, globalization increases inequality within a nation but decreases inequality between nations [54]. It can therefore be argued that the benefits of globalization have not reached everyone equally. There are also mixed relationships between income inequality and globalization with some countries seeing the benefit of globalization while others have not [55]. Statistical analyses have shown that social spending may not necessarily cushion the impact of inequality brought about by globalization [55]. Overall, better approach to globalization is needed to ensure that inequality does not rise due to globalization and outweigh its positive effects.

5. KNOWLEDGE GAPS IN SUSTAINABLE GLOBALIZATION

Extensive and rigorous research is needed to understand the interactions between globalization and sustainability. The foremost question is whether globalization can be made sustainable. This chapter assumes that globalization can be made sustainable based on the synthesis of existing literature as mentioned in preceding sections and the author's reflection. However, if future studies and empirical evidence categorically confirm that sustainable globalization is not possible, alternative models to globalization need to be investigated.

In order to tackle a complex question of whether globalization can be made sustainable or not, the following three unanswered questions need to be addressed:

5.1 How do big tech companies impact sustainability in the context of globalization?

Globalization allows multinational corporations, especially the big tech companies such as Google, Amazon, Facebook, Apple, and Microsoft (GAFAM) to have global influence and strongly affect environmental, economic, and social dimensions of global sustainability. From environmental standpoint, the big tech companies provide assistance to mining of fossil fuels through artificial intelligence and cloud technologies as previously reported by the author [56]. Cloud technology can reduce complexity of information collection and control time in the petroleum production processes. Likewise, artificial intelligence can improve the accuracy of identifying oil fields for effective mining. The assistance of big tech companies to fossil fuel industry raises questions about their commitment to renewable energy transition. On the other hand, GAFAM also have a potential to greatly facilitate renewable energy transition by the application of artificial intelligence and cloud computing. For instance, machine learning could improve the predictability of intermittent renewable energy resources. How should the GAFAM support environmental sustainability in a globalized world needs to be investigated thoroughly.

From economic sustainability viewpoint, the GAFAM could monopolize global markets of intangible assets and digital services [57] threatening economic sustainability. Intangible assets such as intellectual properties and services play major role in today's global economy [58]. Another very important intangible asset is personal data of global population that GAFAM possess [59]. The GAFAM have been referred to as data-driven intellectual monopolies [57] as they have huge control over digital services and personal data of the global market. Their monopolization and opaque practices could severely harm small and local businesses [60]. On the other hand, the GAFAM have helped the booming of mobile software industry, created avenues for advertisers and ushered in a new generation of entrepreneurs including influencers, podcasters, and marketing experts [61]. Increased globalization will allow GAFAM to penetrate global market more strongly, and the impacts this will have on economic sustainability need to be examined.

Big tech companies also have massive impacts on social dimension of sustainability, particularly on quality of life, freedom, privacy, and equality. Lawsuits have been filed against several big tech companies [59] for possibly maintaining monopoly illegally. There are also testimonials from small and local businesses about how they fear Google more than the Government [60]. For instance, the Government could place limited amount of fine on a small business with minimal impact, but delisting from advertising by Google could mean that the business could go bankrupt, particularly given Google's dominant market share on Internet searches. The arbitrary control of GAFAM over small businesses [60] could therefore lead to unemployment and freedom to independently run business. This could also greatly increase inequality where few people running the GAFAM have control on large population, and globalization could exacerbate this problem by allowing GAFAM to control more people than they already do. On the other hand, the big tech companies can also allow voices of common people to reach global audience and thereby empower people.

Privacy is another major threat to social sustainability posed by the GAFAM. They have contributed to global surveillance for US National Security Agency [57], and loss of privacy is a major concern with GAFAM. Globalization could enable the GAFAM to surveille more people around the world.

5.2 What is the role of globalization in the context of green growth versus degrowth debate?

Another important theme that needs detailed investigation is the role of globalization in advancing the green growth versus degrowth debate. For instance, can globalization support green growth model? Renewable energy and technology play central role in enabling green growth. Globalization could enhance the diffusion of technologies that reduce environmental pressures, but it is yet to be proven that growth can be universally sustained indefinitely. Therefore, a case for degrowth in high-income nations can be made, and it is necessary to understand how globalization could enable degrowth. Overall, it is necessary to investigate how globalization could enable the conflicting economic models of growth and degrowth in order to advance the green growth versus degrowth debate.

5.3 How can globalization maximize its benefits uniformly to environmental, social, and economic dimensions of sustainability?

While globalization may have helped the economic growth of many low- and middle-income nations, globalization may also have contributed to increasing inequality within countries. Likewise, there is a perception that globalization is a threat to national sovereignty [62]. It has also been argued that globalization increases the propensity of obesity, particularly among women, in low- and middle-income nations [63]. From an environmental viewpoint, a study of 130 countries [64] found no significant relationship between globalization and environmental footprint.

All in all, there are positive as well as negative impacts of globalization, and further research is needed to investigate models of globalization that enhance environmental, economic, and social pillars of sustainability holistically.

6. APPROACH FOR SUSTAINABLE GLOBALIZATION

It may not be possible to generalize the degree of globalization that is sustainable, and it is very likely that different countries need different degrees of globalization for sustainability. However, few basic principles could be adopted to decide on the degree of globalization as guidelines. This section proposes such guidelines as below for social, environmental, and economic dimensions of sustainability. A need for holistic approach is also highlighted.

6.1 Social sustainability guidelines

There are several crucial aspects [65] of social sustainability such as human rights, equity, justice, democracy, and health and safety that cannot be compromised. Adoption of any element of globalization should not negatively impact these crucial aspects even if the globalization has other benefits. Since globalization has complex interactions with society, it may not be possible to only have positive impacts from any element of globalization. However, an element of globalization should only be adopted if it has positive or neutral effects on human rights, equity, justice, democracy, and health and safety even if other aspects of social sustainability are compromised for trade-offs.

6.2 Environmental sustainability guidelines

Decision-making on the adoption of globalization from environmental sustainability perspective is not straightforward due to the nature of environmental impacts of globalization. Both positive and negative impacts of globalization on environment can be temporary and reversible. For instance, globalization can initially cause environmental degradation due to economic growth propelled by trade openness and foreign investments, but later lead to improved environment after the population has sufficiently increased average income and technical capabilities, thereby validating EKC hypothesis [66]. However, global study on EKC hypothesis is inconclusive [67] indicating the complex nature of interaction between economics, environment, and globalization. It has also been argued that while political and overall globalization improves the environment, economic globalization harms the environment [66].

In order to decide on the adoption of any element of globalization, it is first necessary to evaluate the immediate short-term and long-term positive and negative environmental effects. If short-term negative environmental impacts are identified, it is necessary to evaluate other benefits of creating the short-term negative impacts. In a situation where it is found that the short-term negative impacts are outweighed by benefits, for example, economic growth, it is necessary to identify future measures to reverse the short-term negative environmental impacts with a concrete timeframe. Therefore, careful planning is required by first evaluating whether the negative environmental impact can be reversed or not. If the negative environmental impact is reversible, the cost of reversing it needs to be weighed against the benefit of allowing it. The element of globalization may be adopted if the benefit outweighs the cost of reversing negative short-term environmental impact.

On the other hand, if the environmental impact is irreversible, it is necessary to analyze if this irreversibility compromises the livelihood, needs, and prosperity of future generations permanently. In a case where future generations need are severely compromised permanently, that element of globalization should not be adopted.

Availability and depletion rates (both in quality and quantity) of critical natural resources are other important environmental sustainability considerations. Although the current focus is primarily centered on reducing greenhouse gases emission by implementing renewable energy systems, the use of critical natural resources by these systems cannot be neglected. Renewable energy systems require huge amounts of rare earths and other minerals such as lithium, nickel, copper, manganese, cobalt, etc., and these minerals exist only in fixed quantities on Earth. A typical electric car needs six times the mineral inputs of a conventional fossil fuel car, and an onshore wind plant needs nine times more mineral resources than a gas-fired plant [68]. From a globalization perspective, it is noteworthy that minerals required by renewable energy systems are concentrated in small geographic areas unlike fossil fuels. For example, the Democratic Republic of the Congo was responsible for 70% of cobalt production, and China was responsible for 60% of rare earth minerals production in 2019 [68]. China alone has nearly 90% share in refining of rare earth minerals [68] such as neodymium, terbium, indium, dysprosium, and praseodymium that are required for solar photovoltaics and wind energy systems. Since critical natural resources for renewable energy are concentrated in small geographical areas, monopolization of the supply chain of these resources by few multinational corporations and nations is a real threat that needs to be addressed with urgency. This is particularly important as major fossil fuel monopolies—BP, Shell, Chevron, Total, Eni, and Exxon—are heavily investing in renewable energy [69]. Fossil fuel industry has held tremendous political power in the United States and globally [70], and if this same industry is again allowed to monopolize the new fuel, i.e., critical natural resources required for renewable energy, what are the implications for sustainability? There is an urgent need to critically tackle this question. All in all, globalization needs to tackle any potential monopolization issues associated with renewable energy systems in order to be sustainable.

Impacts of globalization on plastic pollution and e-waste are another major environmental consideration. Adoption of any element of globalization that increases plastic pollution and e-waste needs very careful cost–benefit analysis.

6.3 Economic sustainability guidelines

Green growth versus degrowth debate is still unsolved, and therefore, every country might first need to rethink whether it wants to follow green growth, degrowth, or another economic paradigm before planning its degree of globalization.

In a scenario where a country chooses green growth, a clear time-bound pathway to decoupling economic growth from environmental pressures needs to be formulated. Environmental pressure should not be measured only in terms of GHG emission but also in terms of air pollution, loss of biodiversity, plastic pollution, stress on freshwater resources, depletion of critical natural resources, land degradation, and other pertinent local pollution. In the context of globalization, a country also needs to decide if it will import products and fuels produced unsustainably from other countries to sustain its economic growth. Economic sustainability cannot be achieved if a country does not produce environmentally detrimental products and fuels on its own country but imports them from other countries, especially from low- or middle-income nations where the products and fuels were produced unsustainably.

For low-income nations with high poverty where rudimentary amenities such as food, water, shelter, and access to basic healthcare are lacking for significant number of people, economic growth propelled by globalization may be adopted even if it causes short-term environmental degradation. This is because if the preservation of present generation is being threatened by poverty and lack of basic survival needs, there cannot be any sustainability or perhaps even future generation. By the same reasoning, poor nations could also adopt infrastructural development enabled by globalization even if there is a short-term environmental damage although it may not be possible to compromise potential long-term and irreversible environmental degradation. It may be noted here that the author is not advocating for short-term reversible environmental degradation for poverty alleviation but only opining that this may be permitted as a last resort if poverty alleviation through economic growth cannot be achieved with zero environmental consequences.

On the other hand, high- and middle-income nations need to strongly embed environmental and natural resources protections in their green growth models. Circular economy may allow green growth to sustain indefinitely although this is debatable. Ideally, circular economy is a regenerative system with no waste and pollution. In a linear economy, a product finally becomes a waste, and manufacturing processes also produce wastes that need disposal. Contrastingly, circular economy uses wastes as resources by creating a cyclical regenerative system that can theoretically be sustained indefinitely. It is highly debatable whether circular economy can be sustained indefinitely with zero negative environmental consequence and yet allow growth because a stable system typically remains unchanged and does not grow indefinitely. However, many believe that circular economy can sustain economic growth indefinitely, and the European Union has a circular economy action plan [71]. Even if the circular economy may not sustain green growth indefinitely, it certainly reduces environmental pressures, and therefore, every economic globalization program should embed circular economy wherever applicable.

It could very well be possible that green growth cannot be sustained indefinitely in high-income nations without importing products and fuels that were produced unsustainably elsewhere. Consequently, high-income nations may need to rethink degrowth or other novel economic paradigms in the context of globalization. Social elements of globalization such as tourism, cultural and technological exchanges, and digital services may allow people in high-income nations to maintain existing quality of life without economic growth or even degrowth. For instance, high-income nations could reduce infrastructural development but rather focus on trading digital services with middle- and low-income nations to maintain its living standards. This is an underinvestigated topic, and further research on how globalization could allow the maintenance of quality of life without economic growth in high-income nation is needed.

6.4 Holistic approach

Holistic approach that takes into social, environmental, and economic dimensions of sustainability collectively is needed in order to devise a sustainable globalization approach. Basic human rights and equality are prerequisites for sustainability and globalization should either have positive or neutral impacts on these prerequisites for sustainability. Likewise, globalization should not enable irreversible long-term environmental impacts that reduce opportunities of future generations to prosper or maintain the quality of life that the present generation has.

Globalization cannot be sustainable if one country prospers at the expense of other countries. Therefore, sustainable globalization should enhance water, energy, and food security globally. Additionally, sustainable globalization should empower people and reduce inequality. Although, globalization requires agreements and laws that countries follow, sustainable globalization should not impinge on autonomy of any country. More specifically, sustainable globalization should not allow giant multinational companies and big tech corporations to be more powerful than any sovereign nation as this is a real risk (see Section 5).

It may not be possible for sustainable globalization to only have benefits with no negative implications at a practical level. Hence, trade-offs need to be evaluated by every country to decide on the degree of globalization it can sustainably adopt. To this end, it is necessary to realize that certain aspects of sustainability cannot be compromised. These include social aspects such as human rights, reduced inequality, livelihood, democracy, health, and safety. These also include environmental aspects such as irreversible environmental degradations that imminently threaten livelihood of present generation or reduce the ability of future generation to thrive and prosper. Once it is ascertained that globalization does not negatively impact the uncompromisable environmental and social aspects of sustainability, other trade-offs need to be evaluated. Since the priorities of every country can be different, these trade-offs evaluations cannot be generalized.

7. CONCLUSIONS

This chapter examines the impacts of globalization on sustainability by considering the environmental, economic, and social pillars of sustainability. Globalization can have positive as well as negative effects on different aspects of sustainability, underscoring the complex nature of interactions between globalization and sustainability. There are several knowledge gaps that need to be addressed to make globalization sustainable. These include questions regarding roles of big tech and multinational companies to enhance sustainability, globalization in the context of green growth versus degrowth debate, and better understanding of how disproportionate impacts (both positive and negative) of globalization can be minimized. Finally, an approach for sustainable globalization is proposed by identifying several environmental and social aspects of sustainability that cannot be compromised by globalization even if it offers huge economic and other benefits.

REFERENCES

1. Beumer C, Figge L, Elliott J. The sustainability of globalisation: Including the social robustness criterion. Journal of Cleaner Production. 2018;179:704-715. DOI: 10.1016/j.jclepro.2017.11.003

2. Barnett ML. Book review: Are globalization and sustainability compatible?: A review of the debate between the world business Council for Sustainable Development and the international forum on globalization. Organization and Environment. 2004;17(4):523-532. DOI: 10.1177/1086026604268098

3. Tang S, Wang Z, Yang G, Tang W. What are the implications of globalization on sustainability?—A comprehensive study. Sustainability. 2020;12(8):3411. DOI: 10.3390/su12083411

4. Rees WE. Globalization and sustainability: Conflict or convergence? Bulletin of Science Technology Society. 2002;22(4):249-268. DOI: 10.1177/0270467602022004001

5. Heinberg R. What is sustainability? In: Heinberg R, Lerch D, editors. The Post Carbon Reader: Managing the 21st Century's Sustainability Crises. Healdsburg, CA: Post Carbon Institute, Watershed Media; 2010. Available from: https://mycourses.aalto.fi/pluginfile.php/1159956/mod_page/content/9/Heinberg_WhatIsSustainability.pdf. [Accessed: March 30, 2022]

6. Purvis B, Mao Y, Robinson D. Three pillars of sustainability: in search of conceptual origins. Sustainability Science. 2019;14:681-695. DOI: 10.1007/s11625-018-0627-5

7. Kuhlman T, Farrington J. What is sustainability? Sustainability. 2010;2(11):3436-3448. DOI: 10.3390/su2113436

8. Al-Rodhan NRF, Stoudmann AG. Definitions of Globalization: A Comprehensive Overview and a Proposed Definition. Geneva Centre for Security Policy; 2006. Available from: https://citeseerx.ist.psu.edu/viewdoc/download?doi=10.1.1.472.4772&rep=rep1&type=pdf [Accessed: March 30, 2022]

9. Wendling ZA, Emerson JW, de Sherbinin A, Esty DC, et al. Environmental Performance Index. New Haven, CT: Yale Center for Environmental Law & Policy; 2020. Available from: https://epi.yale.edu/downloads/epi2020report20210112.pdf [Accessed: March 31, 2022]

10. García-Álvarez MT, Moreno B. Environmental performance assessment in the EU: A challenge for the sustainability. Journal of Cleaner Production. 2018;205:266-280. DOI: 10.1016/j.jclepro.2018.08.284

11. Cook D, Saviolidis NM, Davíðsdóttir B, Jóhannsdóttir L, Ólafsson S. Measuring countries' environmental sustainability performance—The development of a nation-specific indicator set. Ecological Indicators. 2017;74:463-478. DOI: 10.1016/j.ecolind.2016.12.009

12. World Wildlife Fund [Internet]. 2020. Available from: https://wwf.panda.org/discover/knowledge_hub/teacher_resources/webfieldtrips/ecological_balance/eco_footprint/. [Accessed: April 01, 2022]

13. Moffatt I. Ecological footprints and sustainable development. Ecological Economics. 2000;32:359-362

14. Fiala N. Measuring sustainability: Why the ecological footprint is bad economics and bad environmental science. Ecological Economics. 2008;67(4):519-525. DOI: 10.1016/j.ecolecon.2008.07.023

15. Dogan B, Deger O. How globalization and economic growth affect energy consumption: Panel data analysis in the sample of Brazil, Russia, India, China countries. International Journal of Energy Economics and Policy. 2016;6(4):806-813

16. Gygli S, Haelg F, Potrafke N, Sturm JE. The KOF globalisation index – Revisited. The Review of International Organizations. 2019;14:543-574. DOI: 10.1007/s11558-019-09344-2

17. Statista. Top 50 countries in the Globalization Index 2021 [Internet]. 2022. Available from: https://www.statista.com/statistics/268168/globalization-index-by-country/. [Accessed: April 04, 2022]

18. The Global Economy. Energy use per capita - Country rankings [Internet]. 2022. Available from: https://www.theglobaleconomy.com/rankings/energy_use_per_capita/. [Accessed: April 04, 2022]

19. Eurostat. File:Material footprint (RMC) by country, 2019 and 2010, tonnes per capita.png [Internet]. 2022. Available from: https://ec.europa.eu/eurostat/statistics-explained/index.php?title=File:Material_footprint_(RMC)_by_country,_2019_and_2010,_tonnes_per_capita.png

20. UNSTAT. Ensure sustainable consumption and production patterns [Internet]. 2022. Available from: https://unstats.un.org/sdgs/report/2019/goal-12/. [Accessed: April 06, 2022]

21. The World Bank. Upper middle income [Internet]. 2022. Available from: https://data.worldbank.org/country/XT. [Accessed: April 06, 2022]

22. Hussain HT, Haseeb M, Tvaronavičienė M, Mihardjo LWW, Jermsittiparsert K. The causal connection of natural resources and globalization with energy

consumption in top Asian countries: Evidence from a nonparametric causality-in-quantile approach. Energies. 2020;13:2273. DOI: 10.3390/en13092273

23. Barger N, Gardner TA, Sankaran M, Patrick M, et al. Direct and Indirect Drivers of Land Degradation and Restoration. IPBES; 2018. Available from: https://dial.uclouvain.be/pr/boreal/object/boreal:207386 [Accessed: April 06, 2022]

24. Lenz NV, Fajdetić B. Globalization and GHG emissions in the EU: Do we need a new development paradigm? Sustainability. 2021;13(17):9936. DOI: 10.3390/su13179936

25. Shahbaz M, Shahzad SJH, Mahalik MK. Is globalization detrimental to CO2 emissions in Japan? New threshold analysis. Environmental Modeling and Assessment. 2018;23:557-568. DOI: 10.1007/s10666-017-9584-0

26. Onifade ST, Gyamfi BA, Haouas I, Bekun FV. Re-examining the roles of economic globalization and natural resources consequences on environmental degradation in E7 economies: Are human capital and urbanization essential components? Resources Policy. 2021;74:102435. DOI: 10.1016/j.resourpol.2021.102435

27. Shahbaz M, Khal S, Ali A, Bhattacharya M. The impact of globalization on CO2 emissions in China. The Singapore Economic Review. 2017;62(04):929-957. DOI: 10.1142/S0217590817400331

28. Dinda S. Environmental Kuznets curve hypothesis: A survey. Ecological Economics. 2004;49(4):431-455. DOI: 10.1016/j.ecolecon.2004.02.011

29. Meng J, Liu J, Xu Y, Guan D, Liu Z, Huang Y, et al. Globalization and pollution: Tele-connecting local primary PM2.5 emissions to global consumption. Proceedings of the Royal Society A: Mathematical, Physical and Engineering Sciences. 2016;472:20160380. DOI: 10.1098/rspa.2016.0380

30. Zhang Q, Jiang X, Tong D, et al. Transboundary health impacts of transported global air pollution and international trade. Nature. 2017;543:705-709

31. Zhao H, Geng G, Liu Y, et al. Reduction of global life expectancy driven by trade-related transboundary air pollution. Environmental Science & Technology Letters. 2022;9(3):212-218

32. Vaughan A. Harmful Air Pollution Now Affects 99 per Cent of Everyone on Earth. New Scientist; 2022. Available from: https://www.newscientist.com/article/2314659-harmful-air-pollution-now-affects-99-per-cent-of-everyone-on-earth/ [Accessed: April 06, 2022]

33. Wan L, Cai W, Jiang Y, Yang C. Impacts on quality-induced water scarcity: Drivers of nitrogen-related water pollution transfer under globalization

from 1995 to 2009. Environmental Research Letters. 2016;11(7):074017. DOI: 10.1088/1748-9326/11/7/074017

34. Yang J, Tan Y, Xue D. The impacts of globalization on city environments in developing countries: A case study of 21 cities in Guangdong Province, China. Journal of Cleaner Production. 2019;240:118273. DOI: 10.1016/j.jclepro.2019.118273

35. Pata UK, Caglar AE. Investigating the EKC hypothesis with renewable energy consumption, human capital, globalization and trade openness for China: Evidence from augmented ARDL approach with a structural break. Energy. 2021;216:119220. DOI: 10.1016/j.energy.2020.119220

36. Joltreau E. (De)Globalization of International Plastic Waste Trade: Stakes at Play and Perspectives. IFRI: Institut Français des Relations Internationales; 2019. Available from: https://www.ifri.org/en/publications/editoriaux-de-lifri/edito-energie/deglobalization-international-plastic-waste-trade [Accessed: April 07, 2022]

37. Tabuchi H, Corkery M. Countries Tried to Curb Trade in Plastic Waste. The U.S. Is Shipping More. The New York Times; 2021. Available from: https://www.nytimes.com/2021/03/12/climate/plastics-waste-export-ban.html [Accessed: April 07, 2022]

38. OECD. What is green growth and how can it help deliver sustainable development? [Internet]. 2018. Available from: https://www.oecd.org/greengrowth/whatisgreengrowthandhowcanithelpdeliversustainabledevelopment.htm#:~:text=Green%20growth%20means%20fostering%20economic,which%20our%20well%2Dbeing%20relies. [Accessed: April 08, 2022]

39. UNEP. Green Economy [Internet]. 2022. Available from: https://www.unep.org/regions/asia-and-pacific/regional-initiatives/supporting-resource-efficiency/green-economy. [Accessed: April 08, 2022]

40. Stoknes PE, Rockström J. Redefining green growth within planetary boundaries. Energy Research and Social Science. 2018;44:41-49

41. Zafar M, Kousar S, Sabir SA. Impact of globalization on green growth: A case of OECD countries. Journal of Indian Studies. 2019;5(2):145-159

42. Hao LN, Umar M, Khan Z, Ali W. Green growth and low carbon emission in G7 countries: How critical the network of environmental taxes, renewable energy and human capital is? Science of the Total Environment. 2021;752:141853. DOI: 10.1016/j.scitotenv.2020.141853

43. Hausfather Z. Global CO2 Emissions Have Been Flat for a Decade, New Data Reveals. Carbon Brief; 2021. Available from: https://www.carbonbrief.org/global-co2-emissions-have-been-flat-for-a-decade-new-data-reveals/#:~:text=The%20new%20data%20shows%20that,will%20continue%20in%20the%20future. [Accessed: April 12, 2022]

44. Hickel J, Kallis G. Is green growth possible? New Political Economy. 2020;25(4):469-486. DOI: 10.1080/13563467.2019.1598964

45. D'Alessandro S, Cieplinski A, Distefano T, Dittmer K. Feasible alternatives to green growth. Nature Sustainability. 2020;3:329-335. DOI: 10.1038/s41893-020-0484-y

46. Guzel AE, Arslan U, Acaravci A. The impact of economic, social, and political globalization and democracy on life expectancy in low-income countries: Are sustainable development goals contradictory? Environment, Development and Sustainability. 2021;23:13508-13525

47. Shafeeq F, Raza SH, Ramzan S. The impact of globalization on quality of life: An empirical investigation for Asian countries. Journal of Globalization Studies. 2019;10(1):97-110. DOI: 10.30884/jogs/2019.01.07

48. Ortiz-Ospina E. What's the Impact of Globalization on Wages, Jobs and the Cost of Living? Our World in Data; 2018. Available from: https://ourworldindata.org/trade-wages-cost-living [Accessed: April 13, 2022]

49. Zankovsky S, Bezbakh V, Inshakova A, Rusakova EP. Social consequences of economic globalization: Experience of developed and developing countries and perspectives of optimization. International Journal of Sociology and Social Policy. 2021;41(1/2):211-223. DOI: 10.1108/IJSSP-03-2020-0068

50. Gu C. Urbanization: Processes and driving forces. Science China Earth Sciences. 2019;62:1351-1360. DOI: 10.1007/s11430-018-9359-y

51. Ha NM, Le ND, Trung-Kien P. The impact of urbanization on income inequality: A study in Vietnam. Journal of Risk and Financial Management. 2019;12(3):146

52. Adams S, Klobodu EKM. Urbanization, economic structure, political regime, and income inequality. Social Indicators Research. 2019;142:971-995

53. Qu S, Hu S, Li W, et al. Interaction between urban land expansion and land use policy: An analysis using the DPSIR framework. Land Use Policy. 2020;99:104856. DOI: 10.1016/j.landusepol.2020.104856

54. Schoder D. Is a Globalized World a less Equal World? American Economic Association; 2018. Available from: https://www.aeaweb.org/research/globalization-income-inequality-trade-policy#:~:text=A%20common%20

narrative%20frames%20globalization,the%20story%20is%20more%20complex. [Accessed: April 23, 2022]

55. Bergh A, Mirkina I, Nilsson T. Can social spending cushion the inequality effect of globalization? Economics and Politics. 2020;32:104-142. DOI: 10.1111/ecpo.12143

56. Pyakurel P. Roles of Big Tech Companies in Renewable Energy Transition. Solent University; 2021. Available from: https://www.solent.ac.uk/news/roles-of-big-tech-companies-in-renewable-energy-transition#:~:text=They%20can%20either%20support%20or,better%20informed%20low%2Dcarbon%20decisions. [Accessed: April 23, 2022]

57. Rikap C, Lundvall BA. Big tech, knowledge predation and the implications for development. Innovation and Development. 2020. https://www.tandfonline.com/doi/citedby/10.1080/2157930X.2020.1855825?scroll=top&needAccess=true DOI: 10.1080/2157930X.2020.1855825

58. Sell SK. What COVID-19 reveals about twenty-first century capitalism: Adversity and opportunity. Development. 2020;63:150-156

59. Surowiecki J. What Does Breaking up Big Tech Really Mean? MIT Technology Review; 2021. Available from: https://www.technologyreview.com/2021/06/30/1026502/big-tech-breakup-monopoly-antitrust/ [Accessed: April 23, 2022]

60. American Economic Liberties Project. The Truth About Google, Facebook, and Small Businesses [Internet]. 2021. Available from: https://www.economicliberties.us/our-work/the-truth-about-google-facebook-and-small-businesses/ [Accessed: April 23, 2022]

61. Auer D. Regulating Big Tech Will Hurt Small Business. Truth on the Market; 2020. Available from: https://truthonthemarket.com/2020/10/08/regulating-big-tech-will-hurt-small-business/. [Accessed: April 23, 2022]

62. Kuepper J. The Impact of Globalization on Economic Growth. The Balance; 2021. Available from: https://www.thebalance.com/globalization-and-its-impact-on-economic-growth-1978843 [Accessed: April 23, 2022]

63. Goryakin Y, Lobstein T, James WPT, Suhrcke M. The impact of economic, political and social globalization on overweight and obesity in the 56 low and middle income countries. Social Science & Medicine. 2015;133:67-76. DOI: 10.1016/j.socscimed.2015.03.030

64. Apaydin S, Ursava U, Koç U. The impact of globalization on the ecological footprint: Do convergence clubs matter? Environmental Science and Pollution Research. 2021;28:53379-53393

65. Eizenberg E, Jabareen Y. Social sustainability: A new conceptual framework. Sustainability. 2017;9:68. DOI: 10.3390/su9010068

66. Farooq S, Ozturk I, Majeed MT, Akram R. Globalization and CO2 emissions in the presence of EKC: A global panel data analysis. Gondwana Research. 2022;106:367-378

67. Shahbaz M, Mahalik MK, Shahzad SJH, Hammoudeh S. Testing the globalization-driven carbon emissions hypothesis: International evidence. International Economics. 2019;158:25-38

68. IEA. The Role of Critical Minerals in Clean Energy Transitions. International Energy Agency [Internet]. 2021. Available from: https://www.iea.org/reports/the-role-of-critical-minerals-in-clean-energy-transitions/executive-summary. [Accessed: April 26, 2022]

69. Murray J. How the Six Major Oil Companies Have Invested in Renewable Energy Projects. NS Energy; 2020. Available from: https://www.nsenergybusiness.com/features/oil-companies-renewable-energy/ [Accessed: April 26, 2022]

70. Natural Resources Defense Council [Internet]. 2012. Available from: https://www.nrdc.org/experts/peter-lehner/big-oils-monopoly-money-ending-1-trillion-fossil-fuel-subsidies-requires. [Accessed: April 26, 2022]

71. EC. Circular economy action plan. European Commission [Internet]. 2022. Available from: https://ec.europa.eu/environment/strategy/circular-economy-action-plan_en. [Accessed: April 27, 2022].

CHAPTER 4

OBSERVATORY OF SUSTAINABLE DEVELOPMENT IN POSTGRADUATE STUDY PROGRAMS IN BAJA CALIFORNIA

1. INTRODUCTION

The research work documented in this chapter represents the systematized efforts of researchers with multidisciplinary approaches and inter-institutional cooperation efforts. The National Technological Institute of Mexico (TecNM Campus Tijuana) through the efforts of the Department of Economic and Administrative Sciences, the Division of Postgraduate Studies and Research, and the Coordination of the Doctorate Project in Administration have strategically defined a line of research on sustainable development of according to the guidelines of the National Strategic Programs (PRONACES) of the National Council of Science and Technology (CONACYT) as a requirement for the opening of new postgraduate programs at the national level in Institutions of Higher Education, to obtain the Recognition of the National Postgraduate Program of Quality (PNPC).

The strategic articulation generated with the Autonomous University of Baja California Tijuana Campus and its Faculty of Accounting and Administration was developed through a cooperation agreement and coordinated work with a research project oriented to the circular economy and the study of sustainable development for the analysis in Small and Mid-size Enterprises (SMEs) in the City of Tijuana.

The postgraduate program of Master in Administration of the National Technological Institute of Mexico Campus Tijuana, with a history of more than 25 years, has become the space and benchmark for applied research in Economic and Administrative Sciences, being the benchmark for intervention models, Unit of Verification of Municipal Development according to the Global Agendas such as the sustainable development goals (SDG), for their respective evaluation and feedback to the representatives of the Municipalities of the State of the Government of Baja California.

The University of Guadalajara through the International Center for Social Innovation for Development has generated collaborative actions of experiences developed in the Municipalities of the State of Jalisco.

The academic link and applied research of the TecNM Campus Tijuana has been characterized by leadership and the convocation of Professors, Researchers, Specialists, Researchers, and Representatives of the Social Sector. The objectives of collaborative work have generated academic and outreach productivity, as well as social economy forums, and sustainable development seminars with interventions by specialists at the local, national and international levels. In order to lay the foundations and cultivate the research line of the future postgraduate program of Doctorate in Administration, a National Research Project is being developed, entitled: Observatory of sustainable development in postgraduate study programs in Baja California. The scientific research project is registered in the call of the Technological National of Mexico. And the purpose is to eventually generate a model that can be replicated at the regional and even national and international levels according to the Global Agendas for raising awareness of sustainable development in the higher education sector.

The circular economy as a term of reference and practice-oriented towards a virtuous cycle of raw materials through recycling to reuse waste has its reference point chronologically since the 1980s. Associating the circular economy with creative initiatives. Likewise, as a point of reflection on the impact of the growing demand for non-renewable raw materials and an impact on the environment and the economy of society. Circular economy (CE), is a new concept characterized by processes associated with research, development, and innovation that challenges the linear economy model that several developing countries, towards paradigm changes in the production processes of waste management. Raw materials, and actions to prolong the virtuous cycle of recycling, reuse, and reduction of raw materials in production processes. Seeking with it, models of culture and adaptation of good sustainable development practices in organizations, and properly in all stages of the supply chain; suppliers, producers, and customers [1].

The development of the research note starts from the prospective of the objective of the scientific research project to lay the methodological bases that respond to the research question: What are the variables to determine the level of culture on the sustainable development goals (SDG)? To build an observatory for the evolution of the SDGs [2] and circular economy under the local territorial approach in the municipalities, from an academic perspective. The documentary analysis of studies at the international level as a reference framework to identify best practices in business awareness and education in the new generations for the development of programs and initiatives to promote sustainable development is connected with the structure of the NODESS [3] model (Development Nodes of Social and Solidarity Economy) that represents the articulation of Institutions of Higher Education, Local Government (Municipalities) [4] and the Organism of the Social Economy (Cooperatives and Cooperative Associations), generating experiences of coexistence and education for life, through the identification of needs, projects and innovation in the city of Tijuana and its metropolitan area; carrying out action strategies that comply with four strategies aimed at 1. Research, 2. Dissemination, 3. Dissemination and 4. Publication.

The work team made up of academics, researchers, municipal officials and members of cooperatives develop responsibility and strategic leadership in matters of research, dissemination, entrepreneurship and capacity development, linkage, follow-up, and monitoring. Through a training and orientation program in the communities on the 17 SDGs and circular economy. This includes a program of meaningful learning practices to promote a culture of awareness of the sustainable development approach that involves three main spheres in perfect balance: 1. Economy, 2. Social aspect, and 3. Environment. And under the methodological practices of systemic focus groups, an inventory of good practices and a catalog of projects that affect the circular economy are developed, as well as sustainable development under the analysis of the contents of study plans aligned to sustainable culture. With the results of the prospective research on the needs of culture and education on circular economy, dictionaries of sectoral competences Dictionary of Sectoral Competences (DSC), in Spanish Diccionario de Competencias Sectoriales (DCS) [5] will be designed that include labor, professional, and research competences, as an empowerment strategy in the different levels of education from basic education up to postgraduate level. Having an emphasis on the importance of transmitting to future generations of citizens in the different sectors of society, from a family father, an entrepreneur, a professional, a government official, or the population in general.

2. DESIGN AND METHOD

2.1 FHS systemic intervention model for SDGs and circular economy

The Fifth Systemic Helix (FHS) Methodology [6] for the analysis of sustainable development and circular economy has been developed on the approach of systemic competitiveness, emphasizing research, development, and innovation; as a sectoral articulation factor. The QHS methodology generates a series of strategic actions and initiatives to achieve public policy [7, 8] initiatives and communication mechanisms that can give continuity to projects, with the aim of having a more developed society with a developing culture and education. Sustainability and the impact of the SDGs, as well as sensitivity to the principles of the circular economy.

The project of a “Social Economy Observatory in Latin America” creates a prospective reflection on the structural conditions necessary for indicators that are the formula to determine the gaps of reality vs. the ideal phase, which generate as a result of the areas of opportunity for each sector of society through the QHS approach [9]. The systemic methodological proposal considers in-depth interviews of the opinion context on local projects and their impact on the sustainable development goals (SDG) and the circular economy [10].

Table 1 presents a series of questions developed as a reflection strategy to create specific actions in the different sectors of society to generate culture and awareness of the importance of the objectives for sustainable development (SDG) and the circular economy [11].

The conceptual definition of sustainable development is argued from three perspectives on the relationship between the environment and economic and social development. The conceptual genesis of sustainable development is based on the principles of allowing the needs of present generations to be met without compromising the possibilities of those of the future, of meeting their own needs and meeting an environmental protection agenda in countries with lower levels of developing. They need development of environmental policies and development strategies in their economic and social and environmental sectors.

Table 1. Bank of questions to determine the SDG and circular economy project.

Focus FHS	Bank of questions by systemic sector
H1. Companies	What are the problems or challenges of the business sector to develop projects and initiatives for SDGs and circular economy? What do companies need to develop programs aimed at SDGs and the circular economy? What are the barriers that companies face to implement circular economy projects? Are companies aware of the best circular economy practices? Have the consultants contributed to implementing circular economy initiatives? What do companies need to open up to educational linkages for the circular economy How can companies be linked with the different sectors of society, to improve the conditions of the circular economy? Do companies consider some type of occupational profile for job skills, professionals, and research on circular economy? How can service providers contribute to circular economy practices in companies? What kind of help do companies need to develop local technology with support from the government and schools to implement circular economy projects? What is the profile of a successful company, with circular economy practices?
H2. Universities	What are the knowledge and skills (competencies) provided in the Schools for SDGs and circular economy? How do Universities update their study plans and programs in accordance with the advances and development of the SDGs and the circular economy? How are teachers updated to teach the current issues of SDGs and circular economy? How do you measure the effectiveness of your study programs, according to the SDG and circular economy development indicators? How is the link between the education sector and companies promoted to develop SDG and circular economy projects?

H3. Government	What are the government programs to promote the development of SDGs and circular economy? How does the government facilitate the development of suppliers with an SDG and circular economy approach? What does the government need to develop public policies that encourage SDGs and circular economy? What initiatives has the government developed to promote each SDG and circular economy? What strategic actions is the government developing in the short, medium, and long term for SDGs and the circular economy? What failures does the government recognize that it has had to achieve the progress of the SDGs and the circular economy? Is there a local or national agenda for the development of SDGs and circular economy?
H4. Associations	What are the strategies of business associations to help companies and suppliers develop and implement actions aimed at SDGs and the circular economy? What programs have business associations generated and encouraged to promote SDGs and the circular economy? How is research on SDGs and circular economy promoted? How is communication between companies promoted to promote SDGs and the circular economy? How is the certification of labor, professional, and research skills promoted on awareness and culture on SDGs and circular economy?
H5. Consultants	What is missing in educational institutions so that their graduates are more focused on the culture and principles of SDGs and circular economy? What actions are recommended to the government sector to strengthen the business sector and its supply chain, and develop circular economy programs? What initiatives are considered necessary for business organizations and chambers to be a key actor or agent of change in the development of SDGs and circular economy? What are the professional services that specialized consultants should provide to promote awareness and culture about the importance and benefit of developing projects on SDGs and circular economy?

The institutional framework for sustainable development and the green economy and the eradication of poverty, as an idea of a paradigm shift necessary to protect the environment, can also generate new opportunities for economic growth, an important issue at a time of international crisis [10].

Economic Commission for Latin America and the Caribbean (ECLAC) has focused this message from the equality trilogy, in particular on "Structural change for equality: an integrated vision of development" and "Pacts for equality: towards a sustainable future". Table 2 presents the opinion methodological approach to the role of interviewees under focus groups in five phases.

Table 2. Methodological approach of the QHS for SDGs and circular economy.

Phases	Systemic analysis approach
1	Public policymakers; development of instruments to identify and develop models: incentives, cooperation structures, financing of research projects, aid to promote sustainable development and good circular economy practices, through the virtuous circle of waste recycling
2	Experts; people with extensive knowledge and experience to achieve an impact on the objectives of sustainable development and circular economy
3	Business leaders; university–company linkage programs that have professional practical goals, social service, thesis on SDG projects and initiatives, and circular economy
4	Universities; they play a fundamental role in the transfer of technology and knowledge, through research, development, and innovation, articulated with all the needs of the sectors of society
5	Representatives of civil society: Worktables with citizens, they are already the key piece of any city project, or of a country, through their needs, business vocations, and the capacities of the talent trained in the various educational institutions

A circular economy, he added, extends the life of the product, with maintenance, repair, reuse, and remanufacturing, and when it is no longer possible to do any of these things, recover parts that can be reused or, at least, rescue the materials or raw materials. The border dynamics of the region between the cities of Tijuana, Baja California, and San Diego, California, generate a business dynamic called CALIBAJA, in which activities of recovery of parts and materials are developed, with initiatives of a circular economy law in the business activities of the metropolitan region and the international link will provide a regulation that facilitates second-hand trade, initiatives of technological circles, and not leave the responsibility of processing our waste, generated by society, to mother nature alone.

The international reference framework according in Chile there are innovative circular economy practices; such as the case virtuous recycling of cigarette butts, recycling of glass bottles into glasses, development of glasses, using the plastic collected from fishing nets. Likewise, a review and construction of a theoretical reference framework on applied research in SDGs and circular economy as shown in Table 3, is the advancement of good practices documented in academic studies [17].

Table 3. Actions aimed at achieving the SDGs and circular economy.

Country	Best methodological practices	Ref.
Mexico	Systemic model QHS–DCS, QHS–NODESS, for the interaction of creators of government policies, business leaders, representatives of universities, associations, and specialized experts from civil society, to determine the level of culture and sensitivity of actions to contribute to the scope of the SDGs and circular economy, identifying needs for labor, professional and research skills in the sectors of society	[12]
Colombia	Initiatives aimed at promoting extended responsibility between producers, manufacturers, and importers of goods and services, in the comprehensive management of product waste when the final consumer discards them	[13]
Chile	Extended responsibility of the producer, until the end of the useful life of the product; conditioning the management of all the waste generated by its processes	[14]
Japan	Exchange program between industries, promoting continuous improvement practices	[15]
European Union	Regulatory framework that allows the effective use of natural, human and economic resources for its transition to the circular economy model; waste can be recycled to transform waste from one industry into raw materials for another	[16]

International studies of advances in implementing a circular economy at a global level is a complicated task, many rich countries do not want to give up their level and way of life. Poor countries seek to obtain a level similar to developed countries but do not have the resources. Some developed countries promote the circular economy through more artisanal jobs; activities of reuse, repair, remanufacturing, etc., including the substitution of non-renewable raw materials for recycled materials. But the concern is that the energy sources are running out and are very scarce. International statistics suggest that rich countries consume 10 times more resources than poor countries, which implies a culture and sensitivity to spread the principles of circularity.

Adaptation, reuse of used products, encourage recycling. Environmental management systems such as ISO 14001 have the task of demanding this type of change to ensure the sustainability of the resources we consume. Agreements, alliances, and cooperation mechanisms are required to make possible the answer to the great unknown of how the less developed countries will face the implementation of these new infrastructures. Some developed countries have shown interest in supporting fewer wealthy nations; however, it is not enough if the aim is to implement a global circular economy [18].

3. FIELD WORK AND DATA ANALYSIS

According to the UN, the sustainable development goals (SDGs) can only be achieved with strong global partnerships and cooperation. Inclusive partnerships need to be established at global, regional, national, and local levels on sustainable principles, as well as on a shared vision and goals that put people and ecosystems first. Due to the global contingency of the COVID-19 pandemic [19], it is estimated that the world economy will contract by 3% in the coming years, representing the worst recession since the Great Depression. Cooperation actions are necessary to guarantee local recovery, under awareness and culture toward the sustainable development goals (SDG). Highlighting its approach and way of addressing them from the different sectors of society: Goal 1: End poverty in all its forms throughout the world, Goal 2: End hunger, Goal 3: Guarantee a healthy life and promote well-being for all at all ages, Goal 4: Ensure inclusive and equitable quality education and promote lifelong learning opportunities for all, Goal 5: Achieve gender equality and empower all women and girls, Goal 6: Ensure availability and sustainable management of water and sanitation for all, Goal 7: Ensure access to affordable, secure, sustainable and modern energy, Goal 8: Promote inclusive and sustainable economic growth, employment and decent work for all, Goal 9: Build resilient infrastructure, promote sustainable industrialization and foster innovation, Goal 10: Reduce inequality within and among countries, Goal 11: Make cities more inclusive, safe, resilient and sustainable, Goal 12: Ensure sustainable consumption and production patterns, Goal 13: Take urgent action to combat climate change and its effects, Goal 14: Conserve and sustainably use the oceans, seas and marine resources, Goal 15: Sustainably manage forests, combat desertification, halt and reverse land degradation, halt biodiversity loss, Goal 16: Promote just, peaceful and inclusive societies, Goal 17: Revitalize the global partnership for sustainable development.

The sustainable development goals (SDGs) are the heart of the 2030 Agenda; they represent the vision of the future we want. And the need for local and international collaboration through awareness and sustainable culture. The 17 SDGs with their 169 goals and 231 indicators, the Member States of the United Nations have firmly expressed that this agenda is universal and with a transformative approach. The agenda has the principle of common responsibilities and generates mechanisms to build alliances for all participating countries.

The SDGs are universal: they constitute a universal reference framework and will apply to all countries. All countries have pended tasks and all face both common and individual challenges.

The SDGs are transformative: the 2030 Agenda proposes a paradigm shift from the traditional development model towards sustainable development: The new approach integrates the economic, social, and environmental dimensions, sustainable development centered on people and the planet, based on human rights and human dignity.

The SDGs are civilizing: The 2030 Agenda is about leaving no one behind. It contemplates universal respect for equality and non-discrimination among countries, without distinction of any kind as to race, color, sex, language, religion, political or other opinion, national or social origin, property, birth, disability, or any other condition. The SDGs are also a local and national planning tool, as a monitoring instrument in the countries. Contributing to sustainable development, inclusive of the environment, with public policies for planning, budgeting, monitoring, and evaluation.

4. RESULTS

The visible inequalities around the world have been a cause for great concern, since today there are around 828 million people living in poverty in the world, a figure that, like the levels of energy consumption and pollution, continues to increase, because although cities occupy only 3% of the earth's surface, they represent between 60% and 80% of energy consumption and 75% of carbon emissions, according to data from the United Nations Organization. From this perspective, the concept of sustainable development emerges as a complex conceptual proposal that articulates the economic, environmental, social, political, and cultural dimensions, within which issues such as equity, employment opportunities, access to goods of production, environmental impacts, social spending, gender equality, good governance, an active civil society in terms of social participation, among others, considering both quantitative and qualitative aspects of development [20].

Preliminary findings on studies of circular economy and awareness of SDGs reflect a rise in actions and good practices of programs for environmental management at the documentary research level, as well as local initiatives such as the NODESS Tijuana project of the city of Tijuana with strategic links with researchers from the University of Guadalajara, Autonomous University of Baja California and the National Technological Institute of Mexico Campus Tijuana, determining in Table 4, the results of the percentage of involvement and commitment of the different sectors of society.

Table 4. Analysis of SDGs actions, circular economy vs. QHS-NODESS.

SDGs	Variables—Indicators	QHS–NODESS–CIRIEC	%
10, 11, 12, 16	Fund for education on sustainable development	Companies, associations	10
10, 11, 12, 16	Comprehensive supply chain recycling programs	Companies, universities	40
8, 10, 11, 12, 16	Circular economy awareness programs	Companies, consultants	30
17	Strategic sector coordination programs for SDGs of the UN 2030 goals	Government with other sectors	20

5. DISCUSSION AND CONCLUSIONS

According to the findings of the documentary and field research, the greatest efforts intangible facts embodied in agreements, and documented programs are found between the Universities and Companies relationship. Generating the reflection that higher education institutions represent the agent of change in societies beyond political discourse and good business intentions. Education is the engine of the training of new generations and the impact on the culture of sustainable development.

The opinion of international organizations such as the International Cooperative Alliance (ICA) [21] is that there is a relationship between the plan for a decade, the social balance, and the sustainable development goals. Preliminary findings of reflection, there are several aspects in the inkwell of necessary agreements in the different sectors of society to achieve the culture of practices to develop in a manner in tune with the sustainable development goals and thereby generate well-being and mitigate inequality in society and contribute to the improvement of the environmental conditions of our ecosystems that we cohabit.

In Latin America, 50% of solid waste is organic matter, of which 90% is not used or goes to waste. According to the Economic Commission for Latin America and the Caribbean, improving the efficiency and useful life of materials in our region would lead to the creation of 5 million jobs. The circular economy has been raised on the local, national, and global agendas of public policy and private activity. Countries of Latin America and the Caribbean, and other regions in the world. The link between the circular economy and international trade has been little explored. According to the literature review, trade flows of waste, analysis of the circular economy as trade policy. Necessary knowledge and technology transfer design and development of training models, and practical awareness models of the circular economy and the

SDGs, in all sectors of society [22]. The business sector, business associations, and the education sector represent a fertile setting for the development of projects that promote practices for the sustainable development goals (SDGs) and initiatives to implement programs aimed at the culture of circular economy. Likewise, a key aspect is the role of the sector of consultants specialized in projects and applied research, and the government sector through policies and awareness programs from the local government, through the combination of forms of articulation of efforts of the different sectors of the society. Generating and consolidating the sustainability of organizations and society. Positively impacting the economy, social aspects, and the environment. The initiatives and projects on circular economy require international cooperation, alliances between public and private sectors to create knowledge and technology transfer, as a great project of interest not only of speech but of harmonization of definitions and norms and leaderships of unity for the benefit of future generations and the legacy of caring for the environment.

REFERENCES

1. Kowszyk A, Maher R. Casos de estudio sobre modelos de Economía Circular e integración de los Objetivos de Desarrollo Sostenible en estrategias empresariales en la UE. 2018. Available from: https://eulacfoundation.org/es/system/files/economia_circular_ods.pdf
2. ONU. Transformar nuestro mundo: la Agenda 2030 para el Desarrollo Sostenible, Resolución A/RES/70/1. Nueva York. 2015
3. Nodos de Impulso a la Economía Social y Solidaria NODESS. 2022. Available from: https://www.gob.mx/inaes/acciones-y-programas/nodos-de-impulso-a-la-economia-social-y-solidaria-nodess-233732
4. Ecosistema de Desarrollo Económico de Tijuana, Ayuntamiento Municipal. 2020. Available from: https://www.tijuana.tecnm.mx/%EF%BB%BFitt-colabora-en-comision-de-economia-social-del-ecosistema-para-el-desarrollo-economico-de-tijuana/
5. Martinez-Gutierrez R. Methodology of Dictionaries of Sector Competences (DCS), to Design Standards of Professional Competences, Research and Labor. In: Nazir S, Ahram T, Karwowski W, editors. Advances in Human Factors in Training, Education, and Learning Sciences. AHFE 2020. Advances in Intelligent Systems and Computing, Vol. 1211. Cham: Springer; 2020. doi:10.1007/978-3-030-50896-8_46
6. Martinez Gutierrez R. Quinta Hélice Sistémica (QHS), un método para evaluar la competitividad internacional del sector electrónico en Baja California, México.

Revista de Investigación Administrativa. 2012;110:34 Available from: https://searchworks.stanford.edu/articles/edsgii__edsgcl.405170452

7. Martínez Gutiérrez R. Quinta Hélice Sistémica, un modelo para el desarrollo de políticas públicas. Revista Cooperativismo y Desarrollo. 2012;20(101):28-51

8. Martinez-Gutierrez R. Methodology of the fifth systemic helix for the development of public sector policies. Journal of Competitiveness Studies. 2014;22(3-4):147+ Available from: https://go.gale.com/ps/anonymous?id = GALE % 7 CA 427666157 & sid = googleScholar & v = 2. 1 & it = r & linkaccess = abs & issn = 23304103 & p = AONE & sw=w

9. Foundation for the Circular Economy (s. f). Available from: http://economiacircular.org/

10. International trade and the circular economy in Latin America and the Caribbean. Available from: https://www.cepal.org/es/publicaciones/46618-comercio-internacional-la-economia-circular-america-latina-caribe

11. Martinez-Gutierrez R, Solis-Quinteros MM, Sanchez-Hurtado C, Carey-Raygoza CE. Challenges for an observatory of the 2030 goals, SDG and social economy, in Northern Mexico. In: Goonetilleke RS, Xiong S, Kalkis H, Roja Z, Karwowski W, Murata A, editors. Advances in Physical, Social & Occupational Ergonomics. AHFE 2021. Lecture Notes in Networks and Systems. Vol. 273. Cham: Springer; 2021. doi:10.1007/978-3-030-80713-9_24

12. Martinez-Gutierrez R, Solis-Quinteros MM, Ibarra-Estrada ME, Hurtado-Sanchez C, Carey-Raygoza CE, Chavez-Ceja B. Observatory for the Development of 2030 Goals and the Circular Economy in Baja California. In: Ahram T, Taiar R, editors. Human Interaction, Emerging Technologies and Future Systems, V. IHIET 2021. Lecture Notes in Networks and Systems. Vol. 319. Cham: Springer; 2022. doi:10.1007/978-3-030-85540-6_163

13. Castillo P. Diseño metodológico para investigar el estado actual de la economía circular en Colombia [Tesis de Maestría, Pontificia Universidad Javeriana]. Repositorio Institucional Pontificia Universidad. 2018. Available from: http://hdl.handle.net/10554/41653

14. Hoja de ruta para un Chile Circular al 2040. Ministerio del Medio Ambiente, Gobierno de Chile. Available from: https://economiacircular.mma.gob.cl/hoja-de-ruta/

15. Institut Montaigne. The circular economy: Reconciling economic growth with the environment. 2016. Available from: https://www.institutmontaigne.org/en/publications/circular-economy-reconciling-economic-growth-environment

16. Arroyo R. The circular economy as a factor of sustainable development of the productive sector. INNOVA Research Journal. 2018;3(12):78-98 Available from: http://revistas.uide.edu.ec/index.php/innova/index

17. Suazo B. Economía Circular en Chile: Alcances, problemas y desafíos en la gestión de la ley REP. [Seminario para el título de Ingeniero Comercial, Mención Administración. Universidad de Chile, Facultad de Ciencias Económicas y Administrativas]. 2017. Available from: http://repositorio.uchile.cl/handle/2250/146815

18. Economía Circular Global: desafío global en marcha. Available from: https://sig-implementacion.com/iso-14001/economia-circular-global-desafio-mundial/

19. Salud COVID-19. Available from: https://coronavirus.gob.mx/informacion-accesible/

20. Punto de acuerdo para incorporar preceptos de economía circular al Plan Estatal de Desarrollo en el Gobierno del Estado de Baja California, México. Available from: https://diariotijuana.info/2022/01/presenta-roman-cota-punto-de-acuerdo-para-incorporar-preceptos-de-economia-circular-al-plan-estatal-de-desarrollo

21. Monreal R, Bolaños-Cacho R. Iniciativa con proyecto de Decreto por el que se aprueba la Ley general de economía circular. Senado Morena Gobierno de México. 2019 Available from: https://morena.senado.gob.mx/2019/10/28/iniciativa-con-proyecto-de-decreto-queexpide-la-ley-general-de-economia-circular/

22. Alarcón MA, Álvarez JF. El Balance Social y las relaciones entre los Objetivos de Desarrollo Sostenible y los Principios Cooperativos a través de un Análisis de Redes Sociales. CIRIEC—Spain, Journal of Public, Social and Cooperative Economy. 2020;99:57-87. DOI: 107203/CIRIEC-E.99.14322

CHAPTER 5

ITALY'S SMALL EXPORTING COMPANIES: GLOBALIZATION AND SUSTAINABILITY ISSUES

1. INTRODUCTION

Small and medium-sized enterprises (SMEs) have always been the backbone of the Italian economic and entrepreneurial system: they play a decisive role in terms of contribution to GDP formation, employment, and value added [1, 2].

The globalization process that has been underway for some decades, together with the digital revolution of recent years, has pushed many small businesses to accept the challenge of internationalization driven by the search of opportunities for affirmation and growth. The analysis of this phenomenon must start from a definition of the concept of internationalization. In order to underline the complexity of the theme and its evolution over time, it is possible to refer to the following quotes: Johanson and Vahlne define internationalization "as a process in wich a firms steps up in incremental stages its involvement in international operations" [3], while Calof and Beamish consider internationalization "as the process of adapting a firm's operations (strategy, structure, resource, etc.) to international environments" [4].

Data on the European economic system show that, although small enterprises represent on average more than 95% of the total number of enterprises, their contribution to import-export activities is significantly lower than the one offered by large enterprises and varies between 20% and 40%. There is, undoubtedly, a greater propensity for large companies to internationalize, considering that, on average, 90% of large companies export their products, while only a small share of SMEs (between 10% and 25%) sell across borders [5]. The Italian situation appears more favorable than that of other European countries: it is characterized by a significant contribution of small enterprises to international trade (exceeding in a few years the value of import-export achieved by large enterprises) and by a steady growth in the number of companies choosing to internationalize [6].

The European Union (EU) also recognizes the strategic importance of the internationalization process for the development of SMEs and tends to promote this process through various economic policy instruments, such as the Communications "Small Business, Big Word" [7], or "Trade, Growth and World Affaires. Trade policy as a core component of the EU's 2020 strategy" [8].

Despite the obvious advantages of import-export activities in terms of turnover growth and consolidation of international competitive position, the choice to operate outside the national borders involves some difficulties. The high costs of managing orders, the complexity of bureaucratic procedures, and the need for qualified personnel are some of the problems that small businesses have to face in order to undertake an internationalization process. It is also important to underline the presence of financial constraints to which SMEs are traditionally subject, such as equity gap, information opacity, excessive debt weight in the financial structure [9]: about financial aspect, internationalized companies must also deal with the lack of working capital to support the necessary investments in global markets and to finance exports. These issues can discourage small business and slow down their internationalization process.

In this perspective, the present research work aims to analyze the financial and economic situation of small Italian exporting companies in the period between 2011 and 2020 selected from the AIDA database. The results obtained by applying some indicators to the reclassified financial statements of small exporting companies were then compared with the values obtained by applying the same indicators to all small Italian companies, selected from the same database. The objective is to verify the health of small exporting enterprises, analyzing their strengths and weaknesses, as well as to compare it with the situation of non-exporting ones, assessing the nature and extent of any differences in performance levels.

The research work is organized as follows. Paragraph 2 offers a review of the literature on the opportunities and limitations associated with a choice of internationalization of SMEs. The third paragraph defines the research methodology and exposes the results obtained, while the subsequent section proposes a reasoned discussion on the causes and dynamics that led to the formation of the same results. The last section contains the conclusions and outlines issues for further discussion.

2. LITERATURE REVIEW

As stated above, previous research suggests that SMEs in Italy drive most of the export value but represent a very small number of the total amount of exporting firms [10, 11]. The Italian productive structure is in fact characterized by numerous small enterprises, which, individually, do not influence export performance, but which, in aggregate, have a significant growth potential. For this reason, our attention is focused in this paragraph on the challenges and barriers that hinder the internationalization, first in general of SMEs and then in particular of small Italian enterprises.

As compared with the large enterprises, SMEs are potentially elastic and flexible and benefit from a fast decision-making process, but they often suffer from a top management characterized by poor skills, little dynamism and motivation, limited ability to interpret economic and social changes, and low propensity to accept risk and to update and innovate their business. These characteristics play an important role in the growth path of a company and are crucial in the process of internationalization. On the other hand, larger firms, being well skilled and motivated, respond better than SMEs to the challenges of internationalization and can gain a competitive advantage in foreign markets thanks to the economies of scale and scope inherent in their size and to the financial and technological resources at their disposal. The experience and *global mindset* of their managers often lead to the establishment of export departments or to foreign direct investment, such as foreign-located structures, to conduct export activities on a more solid basis. These are more difficult to realize for small companies, because they lack both financial and human resources involved in these projects.

Given limited resources, the internationalization process of SMEs differs significantly from that of large enterprises and already-established multinationals. Paul, Parthasarathy and Gupta [12] and Vernon [13] report that some firms introduce new products in their home market to gather information and learn from their performance, then expand their offering by starting with export and later venturing into foreign direct investments. This is usually done in multinational companies. SMEs, on the other hand, generally adopt a process that pays more attention to *psychic distance*, choosing foreign markets whose language, culture, and political system do not differ substantially from their own.

Among the factors that help the internationalization process of SMEs, Mitgwe [14] emphasizes the importance of network relationships as a source of information and knowledge about foreign markets. Hessel and Parker [15] point out that affordability, independence, and flexibility are the key factors motivating SMEs to follow the network approach theory, especially when they do not already have a presence abroad. Moreover, SMEs constrained by limited resources are likely to value informal collaborations, which are cheaper than formal ones and, most importantly, do not entail the loss of control by ownership and managers.

Cavusgil and Knight [16] describe the path followed by some companies that internationalize soon after their inception, highlighting their ability to innovate and create new knowledge and capabilities. These companies are called International New Ventures (INVs) or Born Global. Their managers are leaders and have an effective market orientation. This is typical of high-tech companies that are able to convert new technology into commercial success. It is clear that the factors influencing the internationalization of small enterprises are manifold and may be specific to the individual firm, the industry it belongs, or the country it is in, or may result from existing trade rules and domestic regulations of foreign countries.

2.1 Economic and cultural barriers to internationalization

The literature classifies export barriers as internal or external factors depending on the control the firm has over them. Internal factors are intrinsic to the firm and are associated to the lack of qualified and competent personnel needed to administer export activities [17] as well as creative owners and managers able to design and sustain the export strategy. Exporting requires managers and senior executives to have an entrepreneurial dynamism and an international orientation. Many researchers, such as Felício, Caldeirinha and Rodrigues [18], Gupta and Govindarajan [19], Kyvik [20], call this attitude *global mindset*. It is the ability to understand global scenarios and trends, foreign markets and institutions in order to identify opportunities and threats, reshape perceptions about psychic distance and barriers, learn from experience, and improve organization and operations to better support internationalization. Small companies lack experience in export activities and therefore perceive a higher incidence of impediments in going international than companies having more experience [21]. Cadogan, Diamantopoulos and Siguaw [22], and Reuber and Fischer [23] found that experience in international business is an essential factor in overcoming and addressing export barriers. Furthermore, according to Ganotakis and Love [24], a distinction must be made between the human capital skills required to enter foreign markets—the managerial motivation and orientation toward international markets—and those required operationally to achieve and sustain export success. They note that small firms may find it difficult to attract the full range of such diverse skills because they are not available in their domestic market, or because small firms cannot afford to sufficiently compensate workers. Gomez-Mejia [25] showed that exporting companies, on the other hand, may be able to offer more favorable conditions to their employees than non-exporters in terms of monetary (higher salary) and non-monetary (status, travel, and work environment) rewards. Suárez-Ortega and Álamo-Vera [26] added knowledge of foreign language, exposure to foreign culture, and missing training among the factors that negatively influence internationalization. Training and learning practices are important aspects of managing export operations, but many researchers [27, 28, 29] have found that, in general, small firms are very skeptical about the benefit of such initiatives and their managers hardly comply with qualifications and requirements, the use of performance appraisal and competitive compensation, and unlikely promote a learning culture and learning capabilities.

The literature shows that even regular exporters face problems in export transactions, having to cope with the so-called *disadvantage of foreignness* [30, 31, 32]. This is due to their being less familiar than domestic competitors with conditions and conventions prevailing in foreign markets. Wu, Sinkovics, Cavusgil and Roath [33] focused on the benefits from foreign distributors and found that trust, knowledge sharing, and contract-based relationships are useful mechanisms to overcome lack of foreign market expertise, manage relationships, and mitigate distributor opportunism. The importance of external support is clearly seen in a multiple case study made by Haag, Sallnäs and Sandberg [34]. All case companies have hired external lawyers and staff or used external promotion organizations and logistics providers for supplying the foreign markets. All case companies have integrated external support into their organization by obtaining market-specific knowledge (customer behavior, competitors' choices, dominant culture) and guidance on export procedures and routine definition. Moreover, all case companies have used a trial-and-error approach and learned from external support and experience to improve organization and operations. Experiential learning is found, in particular, in the logistics organization. For example, companies have learnt from experience that logistic operations should be centralized in order to increase the in-house control and supply foreign markets more efficiently. Also, the warehouse operations should be standardized to achieve better control on the product flow to foreign markets.

2.2 Financial constraints to internationalization

Developing external support and rapidly improving organizations can be expensive and perhaps beyond the financial reach of small enterprises. Much research points out that the financing of export-related expenses is one of the main internal obstacles for small enterprises [29, 35, 36]. In particular, the literature on international trade signals the presence of *sunk entry costs*, i.e., fixed costs to be paid upfront, such as legal advisory services, foreign market analysis, adaptation of products and services to meet the regulations and demand of the new market, channels selection and setting up, translation of documents, travel expenses. These are often intangible or firm-specific assets, with no salvage value because they cannot simply be traded on other markets. The existence of sunk entry costs raises the question of financing such expenses, which, by their nature, are not matched by contemporaneous revenues. Only companies that manage to overcome this financial problem can become exporters.

Several empirical studies [29, 37, 38, 39, 40, 41] show that small firms have to rely more on self-financing, using retained earnings, and that constrained firms need to cut costs according to the availability of internal financing.

It is widely acknowledged that SMEs suffer from information asymmetry and higher agency costs than large firms. Serious imperfections exist in both equity and debt markets. In equity markets, initial public offerings of small companies are subject to higher underpricing, and listing is relatively more expensive to organize for small issues [42, 43]. Furthermore, SMEs' owners and managers are reluctant to sell equity to third parties and give up independence and control [30, 44]. The same applies for business angel and venture capital finance. In addition, monitoring of SMEs is more difficult and expensive as they have a lower credit history as well as reputation and are subject to less rigorous reporting requirements than large firms. Therefore, SMEs are also not very attractive for business angels and venture capitalists.

As a consequence of this *equity gap*, small firms are more dependent on bank debt, trade credit, and owner loans [37, 38]. Bank financing is the most common source of funding, although for small firms banks may ration credit rather than raise interest rates to overcome information asymmetry. In perfect markets, all valuable projects should be financed, but export projects and foreign direct investments are characterized by highly variable returns and the assessment of their future incomes and cash flows is often unfeasible for banks. Collateralization may help mitigate credit rationing, but these projects frequently involve, as stated above, intangible assets with little or no collateral value. Therefore, even for companies with promising growth opportunities, it is extremely difficult to raise external capital on reasonably favorable terms. Binks and Ennew [45] observe that SMEs are dissatisfied with the quality of service provided by their banks and generally perceive their banking relationship as poor. From interviews with small businesses, De Maeseneire and Claeys [38] found that banks only lend for acquiring fixed assets and not for any market studies or advisory services and that obtaining financing is a time-consuming process. It is therefore not surprising, as Bellone, Musso, Nesta and Schiavo [35] argue, that firms starting to export exhibit a significant ex-ante financial advantage over their non-exporting counterparts. Thus, financial constraints prevent firms from selling abroad: firms that are unable to secure sufficient internal funds or access external funds may not be able to serve foreign markets.

2.3 Exogenous problems to internationalization

External barriers to internationalization are in addition to internal ones. They are caused by factors beyond the control of the company and are often categorized as macro or exogenous problems. Many studies [12, 15, 46, 47, 48, 49] have found that the domestic business environment has a significant effect on export projects, compared with the firm's competencies and industry factors. The main barriers are related to domestic regulations, the diversity of the economic and operating environment at the subnational or regional level, the lack of adequate trade institutions and government support, the absence of a stimulating national export policy, bureaucratic rigidity, and administrative practices. Additionally, firms may be forced to accept institutional and cultural conditions in foreign markets as contextual data, without any negotiating power. These include tariffs, quotas, currency restrictions, import and export formalities and controls, custom procedures, and sometimes even the political instability of foreign countries. Another major obstacle of small firms is compliance with certain foreign technical standards and certifications (i.e., non-tariff measures): meeting technical requirements is often time-consuming for SMEs, which also cannot spread fixed compliance costs over large export values. Furthermore, labeling requirements that vary from country to country, and the protection of intellectual property right, geographical indications, and protected destination of origin, although essential in food industry, can have a negative impact on exports [50, 51].

However, the world economy is gradually becoming more integrated as regulatory barriers continue to decrease and technology continues to advance. The admission of new Member States from Eastern Europe into the EU has provided growth opportunities for EU SMEs: the consumer market is now larger and barriers to doing business across borders have decreased. Several EU policy initiatives are already helping European SMEs to reach international markets also outside the EU [52, 53]. These include, for instance, Free Trade Agreements, which facilitate access outside the EU by eliminating protective tariffs abroad or reducing the cost of non-tariff measures.

3. THE METHODOLOGY

The empirical analysis has been conducted on Italian small enterprises. Recommendation No. 2003/361/EC states that, within the SME category, a small enterprise employs fewer than 50 persons and its annual turnover or annual balance sheet total does not exceed € 10 million. Micro-enterprises (with less than

10 employees) have been excluded from the analysis because they adopt simplified accounting that does not allow in-depth investigations.

The financial statements of the small enterprises were extracted from the AIDA (Bureau van Dijk) database and were divided into two samples: companies engaged in import-export activities, consisting of 1,982 companies[2]; companies trading only within national borders, consisting of 42,277 companies.

Many changes have taken place during this period. The first years of the period analyzed (2011-2014) were the closing years of the severe financial crisis that began in 2009. In the following years, until 2020, there was an economic recovery, while in 2020 the pandemic began, which continues still in 2022. As mentioned above, the research aims to compare the financial and economic situation of small exporting companies with that of small non-exporting companies, highlighting the nature and extent of any discrepancies.

The research covers a period of 10 years, from 2011 to 2020. Many changes took place during this period. The first years of the analyzed period (2011–2014) are the closing years of the severe financial crisis that began in 2009. In the following years, until 2020, there is an economic recovery, while in 2020 the pandemic begins, which still continues in 2022. As already stated, the research aims to compare the financial and economic situation between small exporting companies and non-exporting companies of small exporting companies with the financial and economic situation of small non-exporting companies, highlighting the nature and size of any discrepancies.

In particular, the analysis is aimed at deepening four dimensions:

- ☆ investments and growth;
- ☆ profitability;
- ☆ financial structure;
- ☆ liquidity.

Table 1 shows the set of indicators selected for each dimension investigated.

The main results that emerged from the survey are listed below.

3.1 Results on investments and growth

The first aspect to focus on when dealing with internationalization is the company's investment and growth expectations.

It is evident that the choice of expanding the commercial activity beyond national borders requires efforts in terms of new investments, especially with reference to the working capital. On the other hand, however, the empirical evidence confirms that small internationalized enterprises have significantly higher growth rates than enterprises that deal exclusively with the domestic market [54].

The results of the indicators applied to small exporting firms and to all small firms selected to understand the dynamics of investments and growth are shown in Table 2.

Table 1. The set of indicators.

Investments and growth	Profitability
• Revenues on a fixed 2011 base (1) • Fixed assets on total assets (2) • Annual rate of change in investment (Δ%Inv) (3) • Asset coverage ratio (4) • Annual rate of change in total asset (5) • Annual rate of change in equity (6)	• ROE % (7) • ROI % (8) • ROS % (9) • EBITDA/Revenues % (10) • Capital turnover (11) • Value added/Revenues % (12) • Value added per capita (13) • Labor cost/revenues % (14) • Labor cost/ per capita (15) • Employee performance (16)
Financial structure	**Liquidity**
• Debt/Equity ratio (17) • Debt/total asset ratio (18) • Debt/EBITDA ratio (19) • ROD % (20) • ROI – ROD % (21) • Structure margin (22)	• Net working capital/Revenues (23) • Average stock (days) (24) • Average credit duration (days) (25) • Average debt duration (days) (26) • Quick ratio (27) • Current ratio (28)

Table 2. Investments and growth, median values.

	2011	2012	2013	2014	2015	2016	2017	2018	2019	2020
Exporting companies										
1	100	97.11	97.89	100.59	104.2	106.55	112.87	115.14	114.17	101.97
2	0.22	0.22	0.22	0.22	0.22	0.21	0.21	0.22	0.23	0.26
3	—	-2.49	-2.7	-2.33	-1.77	-1.57	-0.43	-0.4	-1.61	4.66
4	1.74	1.74	1.74	1.8	1.89	1.94	1.96	1.99	2.02	2.07
5	—	-0.35	1.41	2.61	3.29	3.20	4.97	2.40	0.61	6.65
6	—	3.71	2.88	3.29	5.06	5.15	6.68	6.21	4.62	10.58
Non-exporting companies										

	2011	2012	2013	2014	2015	2016	2017	2018	2019	2020
1	100	98.63	99.13	101.03	104.53	106.88	111.33	115.2	116.2	102.15
2	0.23	0.23	0.23	0.23	0.23	0.23	0.23	0.23	0.24	0.26
3	—	-2.69	-3.13	-2.39	-2	-1.41	-0.99	-0.87	-1.54	0.72
4	1.28	1.31	1.34	1.39	1.46	1.51	1.55	1.57	1.59	1.7
5	—	0.23	1.22	2.03	2.81	3.08	3.84	2.12	1.11	5.01
6	—	3.85	2.85	3.61	5.43	5.34	6.17	5.73	4.99	8.29

The first indicator, revenues on a fixed 2011 base, is calculated as the ratio between revenues from sales and services of each year under investigation compared with the revenues achieved in 2011. However, a sharp slowdown in turnover growth emerges in the last year, 2020, probably due to the effects caused by the global pandemic crisis.

The indicator fixed asset on total asset (number 2), constructed by comparing fixed assets respect to the total invested capital, represents the weight that the fixed assets have on the total investments. Generally, small firms are characterized by a low intensity of invested fixed capital: the data that emerged from the empirical study show a reduced weight of fixed assets for both exporting and non-exporting companies. Although the values for the two types of firms are quite similar, small exporting firms record slightly lower values than non-exporting firms (the weight fluctuates between 21% and 22% for the entire period, with the exception of 2020): this result can be explained by higher investments required in working capital (inventories and credits) associated with import-export activities.

The percentage change in investments between 1 year and the previous one (indicator number 3) always shows negative values for all the companies analyzed (with the exception of 2020), signaling a progressive contraction of the fixed capital invested.

The asset coverage ratio (number 4), constructed by comparing the sum of equity and long-term debt with respect to the total fixed capital, measures the ability of the company to finance the acquisition of fixed assets through consolidated sources of financing (equity and long-term debt), also offering information on financial solidity. Both exporting and non-exporting companies show values higher than unity and therefore positive from the patrimonial point of view, but companies that also carry out activities abroad tend to have higher values.

Business growth can also be measured by observing the annual variation of the entire invested capital. Indicator 5 shows constantly growing values (with the exception of 2019) for exporting companies and on average higher than for other companies. This information indicates the presence of a development trend of internationalized enterprises.

The latest indicator of the growth dimension, the annual rate of change in equity (indicator number 6), presents positive and slightly increasing values for both types of companies: the joint reading of these values with those that emerged for the previous indicator allows us to affirm that the expansion of the total invested capital was accompanied by an increase in equity and therefore from a strengthening of the level of capitalization of companies.

3.2 Results on profitability

Table 3 shows the results of the net and operating profitability indicators.

Table 3. Profitability, median values.

	2011	2012	2013	2014	2015	2016	2017	2018	2019	2020
Exporting companies										
7	5.3	5.1	4.42	5.48	7.27	7.94	9.69	8.57	7.34	5.34
8	4.19	3.56	3.88	4.17	4.28	4.37	4.68	6.64	4.02	3.12
9	3.67	3.09	3.41	3.84	3.89	4.09	4.46	4.13	3.75	3.44
10	1.14	1.12	1.11	1.11	1.08	1.06	1.05	1.04	1.04	0.84
11	6.51	6.08	6.30	6.77	7.05	7.22	7.39	7.34	6.87	6.72
12	25.11	25.29	25.99	26.47	26.51	27.25	27.42	27.04	27.63	27.58
13	58.160	57.520	58.655	60.620	62.100	63.585	65.370	66.400	66.395	60.444
14	16.70	17.41	17.75	17.91	17.86	18.01	17.47	17.67	18.18	18.84
15	39.630	40.240	41.125	41.830	42.135	42.515	42.515	43.005	46.150	41.730
16	6.05	5.84	5.71	5.66	5.72	5.65	5.65	5.77	5.62	5.44
Non-exporting companies										
7	5.54	5.84	4.55	5.59	7.43	8.02	8.6	8.33	7.72	6.09
8	4.17	3.61	3.82	4.01	4.1	4.09	4.06	3.98	3.73	2.84
9	3.5	3.05	3.26	3.45	3.58	3.63	3.65	3.59	3.37	3.1
10	1.21	1.18	1.16	1.15	1.15	1.13	1.12	1.11	1.10	0.89
11	6.49	6.01	6.22	6.41	6.55	6.67	6.68	6.64	6.44	6.11
12	31.37	32.06	32.82	32.91	33.22	33.9	33.83	33.83	34.25	33.54
13	46.710	45.870	47.000	48.000	49.050	50.210	51.140	52.150	52.660	47.210
14	22.3	23.53	23.98	23.98	23.78	24.13	23.92	23.95	24.5	25.23
15	34.570	35.010	35.660	36.180	36.520	37.250	37.795	38.700	39.460	35.850
16	4.53	4.32	4.25	4.25	4.28	4.25	4.3	4.29	4.2	4.15

The first indicator we look at is the ROE (number 7) to interpret the ability to turn equity into profits. We see a decline in ROE until 2013 with respect to both the sample of small companies and the sample of small exporting companies. In 2013, the former stands at the worst value of 4.55%, while the latter drops to 4.42%. Since 2014, ROE increases and both samples reach their best value in 2017: 8.6% for the sample of small companies and 9.69% for exporting companies. Surprisingly, ROE of exporting companies is higher than that of small companies only in 2017 and 2018.

ROI (number 8) and ROS (number 9) have a very similar trend to ROE: they are characterized by a decreasing pattern until 2014, but both samples reach their worst value in 2020. Furthermore, we note that the ROI and ROS of exporting companies are always higher than those of small companies. The same can be seen for EBITDA, here calculated as a percentage of revenues (number 10): exporting companies outperform the median values of small companies by exceeding the 7% threshold from 2015 to 2018.

The analysis continues with capital turnover (number 11) to assess the efficiency with which companies use assets to generate sales. A decreasing trend can be seen for both samples. Their lowest value, below unity, is reached in 2020.

A different trend emerges in relation to value added, expressed as a percentage of revenues (number 12). As the difference between production value and external costs, it identifies the value that capital and labor have added to achieve a given output. This value is increasing, denoting the ability of small Italian companies to make savings in the acquisition of external factors over time. We note that the median values of small companies are still higher than those of exporting companies (by about 6%). This proves that exporting companies bear higher external costs than non-exporting companies, i.e., higher costs for the purchase of both materials and services.

Consequently, our attention focuses on a very important factor for exporting companies: labor. We calculate value added per capita (number 13), labor cost as a percentage of revenues (number 14), labor cost per capita (number 15), and employee performance (number 16). We observe that exporting companies always have a lower incidence of labor costs on revenues. The difference between the median values never falls below 5.5 percentage points in favor of small exporters and grows over time reaching a spread of 6.39% in 2020. While labor costs are lower as a percentage of revenues, the cost per labor unit is significantly higher for exporters, proving that they offer more favorable conditions to their employees than non-exporters in terms of monetary rewards. The difference between the median values grows over time and reaches its highest peak in 2019 with a per capita cost difference of € 6,690. The results of indicators 11 and 14 show that the employees of small exporting companies perform better than those of non-exporters: both the revenues and the value added provided by the individual employee of exporters are consistently higher and grow faster over time than those of non-exporters.

3.3 Results on financial structure

The analysis of the financial structure allows to investigate the conditions of balance between sources and investments, focusing in particular on the level of debt of the company. Table 4 shows the results of some important financial structure indicators.

Table 4. Financial structure, median values.

	2011	2012	2013	2014	2015	2016	2017	2018	2019	2020
Exporting companies										
17	0.49	0.49	0.44	0.44	0.44	0.41	0.39	0.38	0.34	0.34
18	0.59	0.57	0.55	0.55	0.54	0.53	0.53	0.51	0.49	0.47
19	1.64	1.76	1.71	1.68	1.65	1.58	1.38	1.38	1.31	1.19
20	4.13	4.57	4.52	4.3	3.6	2.98	2.52	2.24	2.35	1.83
21	0.06	-1.01	-0.64	-0.13	0.68	1.39	2.16	2.4	1.67	1.29
22	212	277	301	319	412	452	528	534	612	711
Non-exporting companies										
17	0.54	0.57	0.55	0.53	0.52	0.48	0.46	0.43	0.39	0.38
18	0.65	0.63	0.62	0.61	0.6	0.59	0.58	0.57	0.55	0.53
19	7.04	7.12	7.01	6.88	6.77	6.71	6.6	6.37	6.21	5.16
20	4.63	5.27	5.4	5.32	4.69	4.01	3.52	3.31	3.28	2.58
21	-0.46	-1.66	-1.58	-1.31	-0.59	0.08	0.54	0.67	0.45	0.26
22	-14	-5	4	14	30	41	61	76	95	126

From this point of view, the first aspect to assess is the degree of leverage obtained from the ratio between total debt (short and medium to long-term) and equity (indicator number 17). Small exporting companies show steadily decreasing results over the decade, highlighting the ability to reduce debt in favor of an increase in equity. In addition, these companies, in each year, have lower debt ratios than those of non-exporting companies, thus showing less dependence on debt and greater financial solidity.

The next indicator (number 18), obtained from the comparison between total debts and total asset, defines the weight that the debt has in the financial structure and its contribution to covering the investments. The results appear in line with what was stated for the previous indicator: a decrease in the debt burden emerges over the years and, for exporting companies, lower values than for other companies. This confirms the presence of a greater level of capitalization and capital strength for companies operating abroad.

The Debt/EBITDA ratio (indicator number 19) indicates how many times EBITDA must be generated to allow debt to be repaid. The values shown in the table express the ability of small exporting companies to repay the debt contracted in much shorter times than other small companies.

When studying the financial structure, the cost of debt plays a decisive role as it measures the economic effort involved in the use of debt and is connected with the creditworthiness associated with the financed companies. The return on debt (ROD, indicator number 20) is calculated as the ratio between financial charges and total debts and appears higher for companies that operate only in the domestic market: the financial market therefore perceives small exporting companies as less risky than others. In addition, a gradual reduction in the ROD should be noted. This can be attributed to the general decline in interest rates that took place during the years under investigation.

The cost of debt is linked to the ROI, analyzed in the previous section: the comparison between the two indicators defines the "leverage effect" (indicator number 21) that makes it possible to verify whether the investments made by the company guarantee a higher or lower return than the cost incurred for finance them and suggests whether there is room for debt extension. The results obtained by small exporting enterprises are better than those recorded by other enterprises, even in the years in which negative values have emerged.

The structural margin (indicator number 22), obtained from the difference between equity and total fixed assets, expresses the contribution of equity to the financing of fixed assets and also offers information on the level of capitalization of the company. This indicator also shows more favorable values for internationalized companies, with positive and ever-growing values.

3.4 Results on liquidity

Table 5 shows the results of the liquidity indicators.

Given the nature of exporting companies, it is interesting to study the net working capital (NWC), which represents a much more significant asset class than structural assets [55, 56]. It is calculated as a percentage of revenues (number 23) and, as expected, the median values of exporting companies are always higher than those of non-exporters. The median has an increasing trend for both exporting and non-exporting companies and reaches its highest value in 2020 (with 22.72% for non-exporting companies and 29.84% for exporters). The difference between their medians also increases over time, and in 2020, the NWC of exporters is 7.12 percentage points higher than that of non-exporters.

Table 5. Liquidity, median values.

	2011	2012	2013	2014	2015	2016	2017	2018	2019	2020
Exporting companies										
23	25.65	27.33	26.41	27.42	27.74	26.3	26.33	26.71	27.57	29.84
24	59.01	57.94	58.89	61.78	62.22	61.34	60.66	63.88	64.63	69.36
25	106.3	104.71	103.5	102.06	100.43	98.24	98.28	94.78	92.83	98.43
26	99.29	96.63	97.57	95.36	95.09	96.39	98.41	92.57	90.59	95.63
27	1.04	1.09	1.1	1.12	1.16	1.2	1.22	1.21	1.23	1.49
28	1.46	1.54	1.55	1.60	1.67	1.70	1.71	1.75	1.80	2.11
Non-exporting companies										
23	19.97	21.43	22.05	22.02	21.83	21.4	21.05	21.3	21.55	22.72
24	7.65	7.2	7.52	22.55	22.55	18.05	20.77	21.48	22.39	23.32
25	104.98	107.47	109.86	108.11	106.19	104.85	104.66	101.14	98.26	103.72
26	103.16	100.73	102.55	100.89	99.43	101.36	102.91	96.38	92.74	99.55
27	1.02	1.05	1.07	1.1	1.14	1.17	1.19	1.21	1.22	1.43
28	1.29	1.32	1.35	1.39	1.44	1.48	1.51	1.53	1.57	1.81

The analysis is deepened by calculating the average duration of inventories (number 24), credits (number 25), and debts (number 26) of the operating cycle. In relation to warehousing, the results prove that inventories of exporters cannot be compressed beyond a certain level. The median of exporting companies remains almost constant over the years, while that of non-exporting companies increases over time, with a surge in 2014 from 7.52 days to 22.55 days. In relation to the average duration of credits, the results show a decreasing trend for both samples, but exporting companies always collect faster than non-exporters, even if the delay is only a few days. The trend in the average duration of debts is also slightly decreasing, and generally exporting companies pay their suppliers earlier than non-exporting ones. However, the time gap between their medians is so low that one cannot assume substantial differences between the payment terms granted by suppliers to exporters and non-exporters.

Finally, it is interesting to look at the quick ratio (number 27) and the current ratio (number 28). The latter considers the weight of total current assets over total current liabilities, indicating how the company can maximize the liquidity of its current assets to settle its debts and payables. The current ratio of exporting companies is always higher, by about 0.20, than that of non-exporting companies. This means that exporters can easily pay back 0.20 times more than non-exporting firms for each euro borrowed. The difference between the median values decreases over time, from 0.30 in 2011 to 0.17 in 2020. This means that during the last years of the crisis, exporting companies enjoyed more liquidity than non-exporting ones. However, given the high inventories of the former, it is also useful to monitor the quick ratio.

The quick ratio (number 27) measures the ability to meet short-term obligations with the most liquid assets. It is more conservative than the current ratio because it only considers assets that can be converted into cash in a short period of time, thus excluding inventory and other current assets, which are generally more difficult to convert into cash. A result of 1 indicates that the company is fully equipped with exactly enough assets to be instantly liquidated to pay off its current liabilities. The results show that all small Italian companies always have a quick ratio of more than 1, so they can always get rid of their current liabilities instantly. The medians of exporting and non-exporting companies become very similar, but the value of the former is never lower than that of the latter.

4. DISCUSSION

As suggested by the literature [12, 46, 57, 58, 59, 60], the results reported in the previous paragraphs should be read in light of the Italian economic and financial context. This is because country-specific characteristics either challenge or facilitate the propensity and possibilities of internationalization. In particular, the number of companies, their methods of internationalization, and the performance achieved by small Italian exporting companies depend, above all, on the peculiarities of the Italian economic and cultural context.

Regarding the economic and cultural barriers to internationalization, previous research [15, 61, 62, 63, 64] has suggested that ownership and governance structures can influence SMEs' growth and internationalization as they affect the firm's objectives and willingness to take risks. In particular, Fernandez and Nieto [61] demonstrate the existence of a negative relationship between family ownership and export activity. Graves and Thomas [63] find that the managerial capabilities of family firms are inferior to those of their non-family counterparts when expanding internationally.

In Italy, the entrepreneurial system consists of many small enterprises characterized by family ownership and governance. They usually assume elementary structures and organizations and adopt a strategy of market permanence rather than growth and development [65]. These factors inevitably exacerbate cultural barriers to internationalization, also explaining the much smaller sample size of exporting companies compared with non-exporting ones.

Fernandez and Nieto [61] observe that stable relationships of family SMEs with other firms through shareholding or formal agreements aim to promote their international expansion and provide them with the necessary resources (knowledge, information, commitment, experience) proven to be key factors for a successful internationalization process. In Italy, however, family management is usually associated with the absence of cooperation or association with other enterprises and of adherence to organized trade circuits. Therefore, the internationalization process of small family Italian firms is hardly facilitated by a set of formal network relationships that many scholars invoke to encourage and sustain exports [66, 67, 68, 69].

However, Becchetti and Rossi [70] and Mariotti and Piscitello [71] observe that the presence of qualified localized capabilities strengthens and complements the competitive advantage of SMEs, thus favoring their internationalization. They refer to *industrial districts* as socio-territorial entity characterized by the active presence of both a community of people and a population of firms in a naturally and historically delimitated area [72, 73, 74]. In the district, community and business tend to merge. Each of the many firms that constitute the population tends to specialize in just one or a few phases of the production processes typical of the district. In this case, the term localization indicates something other than an accidental concentration of production processes in one place: community and firms are attracted by preexisting localization factors, i.e., the advanced specialized services available to firms, the existence of a *marshallian atmosphere*, and an environment conducive to innovation and learning. Final products cannot be sold only in the district and require the development of a permanent network of links, based on mutual trust and commitment between suppliers, distributors, clients, regulatory and public agencies, as well as national and international institutions. Generally, the target market of the districts is the external, essentially global market. As confirmed by Becchetti and Rossi [70], economies of scale in the provision of export services and informal face-to-face exchanges on foreign markets may improve the export performance of small firms located in Italian Marshall districts.

Therefore, in Italy, the prevailing method of internationalization of small firms is related to the network approach [12, 14], in contrast to other countries where the so-called International New Ventures or Born Global firms are more present [16]. The network approach emphasizes the importance of informal collaborations between firms. Such collaborations have a broader scope than one single task or one single purchase. They are usually based on complementary abilities and reciprocity, as the joint development of product or the co-provision of services. Collaborations may transfer skills, knowledge, and expertise between firms, but not control and power over partners and their resources. Collaborations are not based on a comprehensive written agreement, but rather on trust and commitment. This rarely provides complete protection against opportunistic behavior. On the other hand, informal collaborations allow partners to maintain considerable independence, which is an important aspect for many family Italian businesses. In addition, informal collaborations may not entail high transaction, monitoring, and enforcement costs, preventing firms from exporting.

As regards financial constraints to internationalization, it is useful to point out that Italy's financial environment is the same as continental Europe's: a bank-based system, with relatively underdeveloped capital markets and a rather immature business angel and venture capital industry compared with those of Anglo-Saxon countries [38].

In Italy, bank financing remains the most widespread source of funding. Therefore, small Italian companies have a high financial dependency on the banking system [75]. According to Del Giudice, Della Peruta and Carayannis [76], this is due to several factors, such as the abundance of loans granted in the past and the traditional ability of Italian banks to meet the financial needs of firms.

Nevertheless, the last two decades have been characterized by a gradual disengagement of banks in the provision of funds, due to the financial crisis. This aspect, combined to a limited financial culture within small firms in terms of alternative financial instruments to banking ones, puts their internationalization projects at a disadvantage, preventing them from realizing their full growth potential. In fact, the volatility of returns, the additional risks, the intangibility of assets, and the informational problems that foreign projects involve result in the inability of the financial market to finance the internationalization process.

Specifically, for a typical Italian family-owned SME, raising equity from existing shareholders is not always feasible, while entering equity from new external shareholders is often undesirable. New financial instruments such as commercial papers, mini-bond, debt funds, crowdfunding, hybrid debt securities are not well known. Although they represent a mean to cover financial needs, they are not yet considered in the corporate financial strategy. As a result, small Italian enterprises facing financial constraint prefer to internationalize in less capital-intensive ways, i.e., they prefer to export rather than opt for foreign direct investments, relying more on self-financing, short-term bank loans, trade credit, and owner loans [39, 77].

Essentially they cut costs to generate the resources they cannot raise on financial markets [78] and use cash flows from the initial stages to finance subsequent export transactions.

In this context, public intervention can be called upon to help efficient but constrained small firms expand their activity abroad [48, 49]. UE policy aims either at lowering sunk costs of entering foreign markets or at reducing financial market imperfections by means of local, regional, or national authorities, or financial intermediaries such as banks and venture capital funds. Italy has spent a lot of public money to moderate equity and debt gaps through loans, interest subsidies, or equity investments. The State does not require collateral or guarantees but can help small firms by guaranteeing their bank loans. An important indirect effect of obtaining state subsidies is that it facilitates access to private finance, by improving the solvency position and providing a positive signal to banks. However, this type of institutional support has received little academic attention, and in Italy, there are no empirical verifications proving the mitigation of the financing gap.

Regarding performance, we find that small Italian exporters tend to be more productive, pay higher wages, and earn higher returns from their employees than non-exporters. Their financial situation also seems to be better: exporting firms are less indebted, more creditworthy, benefit from a lower cost of borrowed capital, and can repay their debt much faster than non-exporting firms. Above all, exporting firms seem to have coped better than non-exporters with the crisis that started in 2009 and ended in the early years of the period under our analysis. This is consistently with the aforementioned empirical literature on the relationship between exporting and SMEs' performance. Greenaway, Guariglia and Kneller [79] observe that exporting can help companies improve their financial health, making them more liquid and less leveraged. Thus, it seems that exporting is a sign of efficiency and a free way for creditors to assess the potential profitability of foreign investments.

Not in line, however, are the results on growth. To capture the different dimensions of the growth process, we measured the growth of revenues, investments, total assets, and equity. We would have expected a better performance of exporting firms compared with non-exporting ones, especially with regard to revenue growth; on the contrary, the median value of revenues expressed on a 2011 basis is always higher for non-exporting firms (apart from the year 2017). ROE is also higher for non-exporting firms (except for the years 2017 and 2018). These results deserve some clarification and reflection.

Many SMEs in almost all counties and industries face growing competition due to globalization and internationalization. Even primarily domestically oriented SMEs must operate internationally to guarantee their competitiveness and viability.

Buying from foreign suppliers is an alternative strategy for developing competitive advantage and enhancing performance [80]. The advantages of this strategy can be manifold. Hessels and Parker [15] mention the cheapness and high quality of inputs purchased abroad or their absence in the domestic market. Thus, foreign suppliers can enable buyer companies either to improve their own products and services or access resources cheaply. This is essential for constraint SMEs. Above all, this is important for small Italian companies.

Italy has a persistent fragility in high-tech sectors and a comparative advantage in low and medium-low-tech sectors [10]. Competitive pressure from emerging countries erodes Italy's positions in the production of final goods, so importing cheaper inputs can help companies save costs and survive. Therefore, in our subsample, there are many companies that only import. Their goal is to reduce purchasing costs and increase profitability, rather than to grow through exports. This reduces the results in terms of turnover growth but improves profitability.

5. CONCLUSIONS

The analysis conducted in this research work aims to offer a snapshot of the economic and financial situation of small Italian exporting enterprises and compare it with that of small enterprises that carry out their activity exclusively within the national territory. The results suggest: the absence of significant differences in terms of turnover growth and investments; the tendency to obtain better economic performance, with higher returns from operations and better performance of workers; the presence of more favorable financial conditions for internationalized companies, especially in terms of debt sustainability; a slightly more favorable situation from a liquidity point of view.

It is interesting to note that many of the indicators examined show anomalous values, i.e., not in line with the previous trend, in the last year considered: 2020. This figure probably depends on the coronavirus pandemic that began in 2020 and which generated an unprecedented global economic crisis. Due to the lack of more recent economic and financial data, this paper is unable to investigate the impact generated by this calamity on the state of health of companies and on the dynamics of internationalization processes. However, the way is opening up for a future line of research, aimed at studying and interpreting the effects produced on small businesses not only by the pandemic, but also by the war in progress since the beginning of 2022 and the consequent political and economic crisis.

The conflict between Russia and Ukraine has brought out all the problems related to the presence of global production chains, causing an uncontrolled rise in the prices of raw materials and generating problems in the supply of energy sources.

These dynamics are destined to affect the balance sheets of companies, especially internationalized ones, which risk compromising the advantages obtained by operating abroad.

A further starting point for an in-depth study of the research concerns the possibility of dividing the samples of the selected companies, exporting or not, according to the sector they belong to. It is quite clear that the current crisis is destined to affect differently depending on the type of activity carried out: this distinction would allow us to understand which economic sectors have been most influenced by the crisis and which aspects of their activities have been involved.

REFERENCES

1. Di Giorgio G, Murro P. Le PMI italiane e la sfida della crescita. Analisi Giuridica dell'Economia Legal Analysis of the Economy. 2021;1-2:3-29. DOI: 10.1433/102773
2. Signorini F. Sulla crescita delle piccole imprese: il ruolo della finanza. 2015. Avaiable from: https://www.bancaditalia.it/pubblicazioni/interventi-direttorio/int-dir-2015/signorini-04112015.pdf [Accessed: April 5, 2022]
3. Johanson J, Vahlne JE. The internationalization process of the firm - A model of knowledge development and increasing foreign market commitments. Journal of International Business Studies. 1977;8:23-32. DOI: 10.1057/palgrave.jibs.8490676
4. Calof JL, Beamish PW. Adapting to foreign markets: Explaining internationalization. International Business Review. 1995;4(2):115-131. DOI: 10.1016/0969-5931(95)00001-G
5. OECD. Fostering greater SME participation in a globally integrated economy. SME Ministerial Conference. Discussion paper. Mexico City: OECD; 22-23 February 2018
6. VV. AA. Internationalisation of European SMEs - Taking stock and moving ahed. 2018. Available from: https://www.kfw.de/PDF/Download-Center/Konzernthemen/Research/PDF-Dokumente-Studien-und-Materialien/Internationalisation-of-European-SMEs.pdf [Accessed: April 05, 2022]
7. European Commission. Small Business, Big World—A new partnership to help SMEs seize global opportunities. 2011. Available from: https://eur-lex.europa.eu/legal-content/HR/ALL/?uri=CELEX:52011DC0702 [Accessed: May 18, 2022]
8. European Commission. Trade, Growth and World Affaires. Trade policy as a core component of the EU's 2020 strategy. 2010. Available from: https://eur-lex.europa.eu/LexUriServ/LexUriServ.do?uri=COM:2010:0612:FIN:EN:PDF [Accessed: May 18, 2022]

9. Pace R. Piccole e micro imprese italiane tra crisi e vincoli finanziari: un'indagine empirica. Piccola impresa Small Business. 2013;1:57-83. DOI: 10.14596/pisb.132

10. Falzoni AM, Grasseni M. Modelli di specializzazione delle imprese esportatrici: Italia, Francia e Germania a confronto. Economia e politica industriale Journal of Industrial and Business Economics. 2012;39(3):89-111. DOI: 10.3280/POLI2012-003006

11. Iapadre PL. Trade and employment in Italy. OECD Trade Policy Working Papers. 2011;126:1-44. DOI: 10.1787/5kg3nh6j2m20-en

12. Paul J, Parthasarathy S, Gupta P. Exporting challenges of SMEs: A review and future research agenda. Journal of World Business. 2017;52(3):327-342. DOI: 10.1016/j.jwb.2017.01.003

13. Vernon R. The product cycle hypothesis in a new international environment. Oxford Bulletin of Economics and Statistics. 1979;41(4):255-267. DOI: 10.1111/j.1468-0084.1979.mp41004002.x

14. Mitgwe B. Theoretical milestones in international business: The journey to international entrepreneurship theory. Journal of International Entrepreneurship. 2006;4(1):5-25. DOI: 10.1007/s10843-006-5872-5

15. Hessels J, Parker SC. Constraints, internationalization and growth: A cross-country analysis of European SMEs. Journal of World Business. 2013;48(1):137-148. DOI: 10.1016/j.jwb.2012.06.014

16. Cavusgil ST, Knight GA. The born global firm: An entrepreneurial and6capabilities perspective on early and rapid internationalization. Journal6of International Business Studies. 2015;46(1):3-16. DOI: 10.1057/jibs.2014.62

17. Yang YS, Leone RP, Alden DL. A market expansion ability approach to identify potential exporters. Journal of Marketing. 1992;56(1):84-96. DOI: 10.1177/002224299205600108

18. Felicio JA, Caldeirinha VR, Rodrigues R. Global mindset and the internationalization of small firms: The importance of the characteristics of entrepreneurs. International Entrepreneurship and Management Journal. 2012;8(4):467-485. DOI: 10.1007/s11365-012-0232-5

19. Gupta A, Govindarajan V. Cultivating a global mindset. The Academy of Management Executive. 2002;16(1):116-126. DOI: 10.5465/AME.2002.6640211

20. Kyvik O. Internationalization of small firms: The importance of a global mindset. International Journal of Technology Transfer and Commercialisation. 2011;10(3-4):314-331. DOI: 10.1504/IJTTC.2011.040893

21. Madsen TK. Successful export marketing management: Some empirical evidence. International Marketing Review. 1989;6(4):41-57

22. Cadogan JW, Diamantopoulos A, Siguaw J. Export market-oriented activities: Their antecedents and performance consequences. Journal of International Business Studies. 2002;33(3):615–626

23. Reuber AR, Fischer E. The influence of the management team's international experience on the internationalization behaviors of SMES. Journal of International Business Studies. 1997;28:807-825

24. Ganotakis P, Love J. The innovation value chain in new technology-based firms: Evidence from the U.K. Journal of Product Innovation Management. 2012;29(5):839-860. DOI: 10.1111/j.1540-5885.2012.00938.x

25. Gomez-Mejia LR. The role of human resources strategy in export performance: A longitudinal study. Strategic Management Journal. 1988;9(5):493-505. DOI: 10.1002/smj.4250090508

26. Alamo-Vera FR, Suarez-Ortega SM. Smes' internationalization: Firms and managerial factors. International Journal of Entrepreneurial Behaviour and Research. 2005;11:258-279. DOI: 10.1108/13552550510603298

27. Carlson DS, Upton N, Seaman SL. The impact of human resource practices and compensation design on performance: An analysis of family-owned SMEs. Journal of Small Business Management. 2006;44(4):531-543. DOI: 10.1111/j.1540-627X.2006.00188.x

28. Matlay H. E-entrepreneurship and small e-business development: Towards a comparative research agenda. Journal of Small Business and Enterprise Develompment. 2004;11(3):408-414. DOI: 10.1108/14626000410551663

29. Moini AH. Export behavior of small firms: The impact of managerial attitudes. The International Executive. 1991;33(2):14-20. DOI: 10.1002/tie.5060330204

30. Leonidou LC. Barriers to export management: An organizational and internationalization analysis. Journal of International Management. 2000;6(2):121-148. DOI: 10.1016/S1075-4253(00)00022-3

31. Morgan R, Katsikeas CS. Theories of international trade, foreign direct investment and firm internationalization: A critique. Management Decision. 1997;35(1):68-78. DOI: 10.1108/00251749710160214

32. Zaheer S. Overcoming the liability of foreignness. Academy of Management Journal. 1995;38(2):341–363. DOI: 10.2307/256683

33. Wu F, Sinkovics RR, Cavusgil ST, Roath AS. Overcoming export manufacturers' dilemma in international expansion. Journal of International Business Studies. 2007;38(2):283–302. DOI: 10.1057/palgrave.jibs.8400263

34. Haag L, Sallnäs U, Sandberg E. Supply chain capabilities for facilitating the internationalization of retailers—A multiple case study of three Swedish retail companies. The International Review of Retail Distribution and Consumer Research. 2019;29(3):321-339. DOI: 10.1080/09593969.2019.1598467

35. Bellone F, Musso P, Nesta L, Schiavo S. Financial constraints and firm export behaviour. The World Economy. 2010;33(3):347-373. DOI: 10.1111/j.1467-9701.2010.01259.x

36. Lu J, Beamish PW. The internationalization and performance of SMES. Strategic Management Journal. 2001;22(6-7):565-586. DOI: 10.1002/smj.184

37. Chittenden F, Hall G, Hutchinson P. Small firm growth, access to capital markets and financial structure: Review of issues and an empirical investigation. Small Business Economics. 1996;8:59-67

38. De Maeseneire W, Claeys T. SMEs, foreign direct investment and financial constraints: The case of Belgium. International Business Review. 2012;21(3):408-424. DOI: 10.1016/j.ibusrev.2011.03.004

39. Giudici G, Paleari S. The provision of finance to innovation: A Survey Conducted among Italian Technology-Based Small Firms. Small Business Economics. 2000;14:37-53. DOI: 10.1023/A:1008187416389

40. Schiantarelli F. Financial constraints and investment: Methodological issues and international evidence. Oxford Review of Economic Policy. 1996;12(2):70-89. DOI: 10.1093/oxrep/12.2.70

41. Ughetto E. Does internal finance matter for R&D? New evidence from a panel of Italian firms. Cambridge Journal of Economics. 2008;32:907-925. DOI: 10.21139/ssrn.1005333

42. Buckland R, Davis EW. The pricing of new issues on the unlisted securities market: The influence of firm size in the context of the information content of new issue prospectuses. The British Accounting Review. 1990;22(2):207-222. DOI: 10.1016/0890-8389(90)90003-Z

43. Lee I, Lochhead S, Ritter J, Zhao Q. The costs of raising capital. The Journal of Financial Research. 1996;19(1):59-74. DOI: 10.1111/j.1475-6803.1996.tb00584.x

44. Cressy RC, Olofsson C. European SME financing: An overview. Small Business Economics. 1997;9(2):87-96. DOI: 10.1023/A:1007921004599

45. Binks MR, Ennew CT. Growing firms and the credit constraints. Small Business Economics. 1996;8:17-25. DOI: 10.1007/BF00391972

46. Child J, Karmowska J, Shenkar O. The role of context in SME internationalization-A review. Journal of World Business. 2022;57(1):1-20. DOI: 10.1016/j.jwb.2021.101267

47. Freeman J, Styles C, Lawley M. Does firm location make a difference to the export performance of SMEs? International Marketing Review. 2012;29(1):88-113. DOI: 10.1108/02651331211201552

48. Landau C, Karna A, Richter A, Uhlenbruck K. Institutional leverage capability: Creating and using institutional advantages for internationalization. Global Strategy Journal. 2016;6(1):50-68. DOI: 10.1002/gsj.1108

49. Torres MM, Clegg LJ, Varum C. The missing link between awareness and use in the uptake of pro-internationalization incentives. International Business Review. 2016;25(2):495-510. DOI: 10.1016/j.ibusrev.2015.09.003

50. Arfini F, Bellassen V, editors. Sustainability of European food quality schemes: Multi-performance, structure, and governance of PDO, PGI, and organic agri-food systems. 1st ed. Cham, Switzerland: Springer; 2019. p. 572. DOI: 10.1007/978-3-030-27508-2

51. Belletti G, Marescotti A, Touzard J-M. Geographical indications, public goods, and sustainable development: The roles of actors' strategies and public policies. World Development. 2017;98:45-57. DOI: 10.1016/j.worlddev.2015.05.004

52. Amiti M, Itskhoki O, Konings J. Importers, exporters, and exchange rate disconnect. American Economic Review. 2014;104(7):1942-1978. DOI: 10.1257/aer.104.7.1942

53. Cernat L, Norman-López A, Duch T-Figueras A. SMEs are more important than you think! Challenges and opportunities for EU exporting SMEs. DG TRADE Chief Economist Notes. 2014;3:1-14. Directorate General for Trade, European Commission

54. Love J, Roper S. SME innovation, exporting and growth: A review of existing evidence. ERC White Paper. 2013;5:1-55. Available from: https://www.enterpriseresearch.ac.uk/wp-content/uploads/2013/12/ERC-White-Paper-No_5-Innovation-final.pdf [Accessed: May 18, 2022]

55. Banos-Caballero S, Gracia-Teruel PJ, Martinez-Solano P. Working capital management, corporate performance, and financial constraints. Journal of Business Review. 2014;67(3):332-338. DOI: 10.1016/j.jbusres.2013.01.016

56. Habib A, Huang X. Determining the optimal working capital to enhance firms' profitability. Human System Management. 2016;35(4):279-289. DOI: 10.3233/HSM-160875

57. Elbanna S, Hsieh LHY, Child J. Contextualizing Internationalization Decions-making Research in SMEs: Towards an Integration of Existing Studies. European Management Review. 2020;17(2):573-591. DOI: 10.1111/emre.12395

58. Michailova S. Contextualizing in International Business research: Why do we need more of it and how can we be better at it? Scandinavian Journal of Management. 2011;27(1):129-139. DOI: 10.1016/j.scaman.2010.11.003

59. Poulis K, Poulis E, Plakoyiannaki E. The role of context in case study selection: An international business perspective. International Business Review. 2013;22(1):304-314. DOI: 10.1016/j.ibusrev.2012.04.03

60. Shepherd NG, Rudd JM. The influence of context on the strategic decision-making process: A review of the literature. International Journal of Management Reviews. 2014;16(3):340-364. DOI: 10.1111/ijmr.12023

61. Fernandez Z, Nieto AJ. Impact of ownership on the international involvement of SMEs. Journal of International Business Studies. 2006;37(3):340-351. DOI: 10.1057/palgrave.jibs.8400196

62. George G, Wiklund J, Zahra SA. Ownership and the internationalization of small firms. Journal of Management. 2005;31(2):210-233. DOI: 10.1177/0149206304271760

63. Graves C, Thomas J. Determinants of the internationalization pathways of family firms: An examination of family influence. Family Business Review. 2008;21(2):151-167. DOI: 10.1111/j.1741-6248.2008.00119.x

64. Zahra SA, Neubaum DO, Naldi L. The effects of ownership and governance on SMEs' international knowledge-based resources. Small Business Economics. 2007;29:309-327. DOI: 10.1007/s11187-006-9025-y

65. Hennart JF, Majocchi A, Forlani E. The myth of the stay-at-home family firm: How family-managed SMEs can overcome their internationalization limitations. Journal of International Business Studies. 2019;50(5):758-782. DOI: 10.1057/s41267-017-0091-y

66. Antoldi F, Cerrato D, Depperu D. SMEs export consortia and the development of intangible resources. Journal of Small Business and Enterprise Development. 2013;20:567-583. DOI: 10.1108/JSBED-04-2013-0062

67. Pongelli C, Caroli MG, Cucculelli M. Family business going abroad: The effect of family ownership on foreign market entry mode decisions. Small Business Economics. 2016;47(3):787-801. DOI: 10.1007/s11187-016-9763-4

68. Roffia P, Moracchiato S, Liguori E, Kraus S. Operationally defining family SMEs: A critical review. Journal of Small Business and Enterprise Development. 2021;28(2):229-260. DOI: 10.1108/JSBED-11-2020-0399

69. Sciascia S, Mazzola P, Astrachan JH, Pieper TM. The role of family ownership in international entrepreneurship: Exploring nonlinear effects. Small Business Economics. 2012;38:15-31. DOI: 10.1007/s11187-010-9264-9

70. Becchetti L, Rossi SPS. The positive effect of industrial district on the export performance of Italian firms. Review of Industrial Organization. 2000;16:53-68. DOI: 10.1023/A:1007783900387

71. Mariotti S, Piscitello L. Localized capabilities and the internationalization of manufacturing activities by SMEs. Entrepreneurship and Regional Development. 2001;13(1):65-80. DOI: 10.1080/089856201750046810

72. Becattini G. The Marshallian industrial district as a socio-economic notion. Revue D'économie Industrielle. 2017;157(1):13-32. DOI: 10.4000/rei.6507

73. Guareschi M, Maccari M, Sciurano JP, Arfini F, Pronti A. A methodological approach to upscale toward an agroecology system in EU-LAFSs: The case of the Parma Bio-District. Sustainability. 2020;12(13):5398. DOI: 10.3390/su12135398

74. Sopranzetti S. The Italian districts in the global value chains. Italian Economic Journal. 2018;4(3):497-522. DOI: 10.1007/s40797-018-0078-2

75. Rossi M, Giacosa E, Mazzoleni A. The financing methods for small and medium companies: Comparison between Italy and Germany. Corporate Ownership & Control. 2016;13(3-2):366-377

76. Del Giudice M, Della Peruta MR, Carayannis EG. Knowledge and Family Business. New York: Springer; 2011. p. 267. DOI: 10.1007/978-1-4419-7353-5

77. Becchetti L, Trovato G. The determinants of growth for small and medium sized firms. The role of the availability of external finance. Small Business Economics. 2002;19:291-306

78. Musso P, Schiavo S. The impact of financial constraints on firm survival and growth. Journal of Evolutionary Economics. 2008;18(2):135-149. DOI: 10.1007/s00191-007-0087-z

79. Greenaway D, Guariglia A, Kneller R. Financial factors and exporting decisions. Journal of International Economics. 2007;73(2):377-395. DOI: 10.1016/j.jinteco.2007.04.002

80. Liang N, Parkhe A. Importer behavior: The neglected counterpart of international exchange. Journal of International Business Studies. 1997;28(3):495-530. DOI: 10.1057/palgrave.jibs.8490109

CHAPTER 6

SUSTAINABILITY AND SOCIAL INVESTMENT: COMMUNITY MICROHYDROPOWER SYSTEMS IN THE DOMINICAN REPUBLIC

1. INTRODUCTION

The origins of sustainable development as a concept go back to the birth of environmental movements in the second half of the XIX century, which began with a romantic emphasis on nature and the importance for human beings to understand it. Its genesis dates back to the Industrial Revolution in England, as an attempt to awaken awareness about air pollution produced by the industries that had had rapid and sudden growth, in the context of a weak legal framework [1, 2, 3].

The discussion about the need of preserving the quality of natural resources joined previous debates on the durability of several raw materials, as well as on the degradation of the environment because of its use. That was the case when there was shortage of certain products and materials or the occurrence of local environmental problems associated with uncontrolled exploitation [4]. Some examples date back as far as Egyptian, Mesopotamian, Greek, and Roman civilizations, several thousand years before Christ, when evidence was collected of deforestation, salinization as well as soil loss linked to overexploitation of land resources in specific areas [4]. In more recent times, we can cite the shortage of wood caused by its excessive use in boat building, which severely threatened Europe in the XVIII century [4].

As a consequence of these episodes, the term "sustainable use" began to appear in forestry, as a way to guarantee the durability of wood exploitation, balancing the cutting of old trees with seedling planting [5].

Additionally, concerns over the excessive use of certain natural resources acquired other nuances in XVII and XVIII centuries, when different authors warned about the consequences of the overconsumption of natural resources, being The Tragedy of the Commons by Lloyd [6] and the Essay on the Principle of Population by Malthus [7] two of the most iconic.

In fact, this new perspective introduced a global vision into the debate, pointing out the existing contrast between a model based on unlimited growth of natural resources consumption and their inherent natural limitation in terms of volumes and times of recovery, not only at a local but also at a planetary scale. In this context, the XX century took place, with an exponential growth of studies that revealed the global climate crisis [8, 9, 10, 11, 12, 13].

Currently, despite the progress made defining a world framework around sustainable development and the assessment of environmental and social impacts, which includes the introduction of new goals [14] and standards (e.g. International Finance Corporation (IFC), performance standards), its implementation remains something difficult to achieve, simply because it is not compatible with the current economic model based on infinite growth and nature's exploitation. The discussion remains focused on profit and return of investment.

To propose an alternate vision, we must reshape the current economic decisions through a wider lens of social, economic, environmental, and political sustainability. This includes a multi-stakeholder approach, where cooperation and synergy at different levels are two cornerstones. Private sector is a key stakeholder, since smart and forward-thinking entrepreneurs are an essential component for the change. They have a key role in identifying feasible ways to reduce environmental impacts and improve life conditions for local people, while working to generate economic and financial benefits [15]. This is possible when companies introduce the environment and local communities into the decision-making process [15].

The Dominican Republic hosts a series of characteristics that have fostered the development of alternatives and new narratives in local climate action, sustainable development, and social investment. The weakness of the Dominican national electric system, which does not guarantee neither universal access to electricity nor continuity of the service, promotes the emergence of alternative solutions which turn into innovative models for local sustainable development financed through social investment and sustained through a multi-stakeholder approach [16].

One of these solutions are community microhydropower systems, which, under the coordination of Guakía Ambiente and the Small Grants Programme (SGP/GEF/UNDP), transform local opportunities and social investment into integral development, based on the empowerment of women and men and the synergy among diverse stakeholders.

This essay discusses the increasing presence of social investment practices by the private sector in these initiatives [16]. By examining the main experiences and lessons learned obtained in more than 20 years of implementation, the document is intended to introduce the case study of microhydropower systems installed in the Dominican Republic and border region of Haiti, specifically focusing on the central role of social investment inside a multi-stakeholder scheme of intervention, as a catalyst of a sustainable model.

The results and conclusions are based on the analysis of technical documents and previous essays, which was complemented with the interview of members from Guakía Ambiente and the Small Grants Programme.

2. DISCUSSION

2.1 Social investment and its link to sustainability

The concept of social investment has changed over the years and has been paired with many other concepts such as responsible investment, Environmental, Social, and Governance (ESG) investments, among others. Multilateral organizations and investment groups have developed their own definitions for social and responsible investment practices. However, most of them are aimed at reducing social conflicts, gaining reputation and maximizing profits in the long term. For example, the International Finance Corporation (IFC) developed the concept of community investing to "help companies gain a social license to operate, access land, reduce project and reputational risks, boost productivity, meet government requirements or global standards, and/or successfully compete for the next venture." [17].

The same approach is used when speaking of ESG funds, where asset managers seek to keep the returns similar to traditional investments and do not necessarily aim at community development and sustainability at a local level [18]. Recovering the arguments from the previous chapter, this article seeks to understand social investment as something that directly impacts positively and empowers local populations, addresses climate challenges, and contributes to a long-term sustainability vision of a country.

The focus of the current document is not to discuss the concept of social investment, and it will use the definition launched by the United Nations Global Compact, which is broad enough to encompass different nuances regarding this complex and widely discussed concept [19].

Social investment was defined in 2010 by the United Nations (UN) as "the practice of making voluntary financial and nonfinancial contributions that demonstrably help local communities and broader societies to address their development priorities." In order for an investment to be considered responsible and social, it must be purposeful, accountable, respectful, and ethical [20].

Additionally, this article focuses on the nonmonetary and nonprofit side of social investing. Private companies, foundations, and international cooperation make these investments for a wide variety of objectives. One of them is sustainability and climate action.

The urgency of actions to address the climate crisis needs creative solutions that do not necessarily give a monetary return to investors. However, there are several proxy indicators that can help to quantify the nonmonetary impact of social investments. For example, the number of hectares reforested and under community watershed management brings general benefits to air and water quality that are hard to express in monetary terms but largely contribute to the climate objectives of foundations and some private investors.

2.2 Community microhydropower systems as social investment for sustainability

In this context, social investors have looked for initiatives that align with their sustainability objectives. In the Dominican Republic, a wide network of community microhydropower systems has developed thanks to these investments. In this section, the article will dissect this model of decentralized community power generation and its links with sustainability and social investment.

Located in the Caribbean, the Dominican Republic is a Small Island Developing State (SIDS) [21], which is highly vulnerable to the impacts of climate change [22], with high inequality and significant levels of poverty [23]. It is also one of the Latin American countries with the highest economic growth considering only the Gross Domestic Product (GDP) indicator [24].

In this context, in 1998, a pilot project of a microhydropower system was implemented seeking to address the lack of access to electricity of 70 families of the rural community of El Limón, located in the Southeastern portion of the Cordillera

Central, the main massif of the country. From then on, the number of community microhydropower systems have grown exponentially in the country: 60 systems of this kind were built in the Dominican Republic and another one in the border region of Haiti, with a total combined installed capacity of 1.5 MW [25]. This ample network of micro-grids gives electricity and empowers more than 5000 households and 20,000 people in climate vulnerable mountainous areas with marginalized populations (Figure 1). In the process, over 70 square kilometers of land were restored and/or are being conserved in the direct and indirect area of influence of the microhydropower systems, while it is estimated that more than 25,000 tons of CO_2 are absorbed and/or their emission avoided annually.

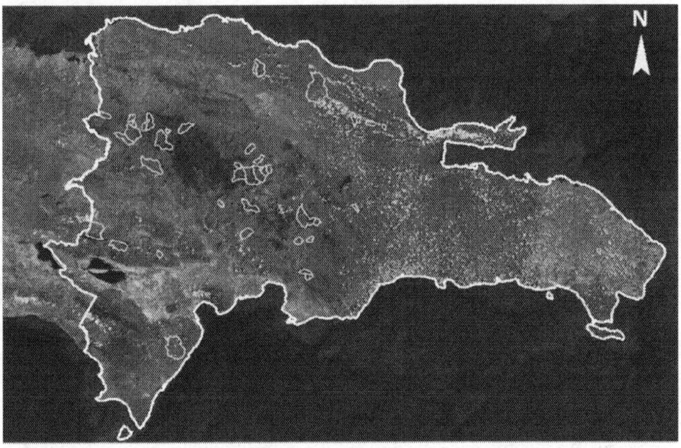

Figure 1. Basins where community microhydropower systems are working [16].

Far beyond being a mere localized project, these systems promote an alternative to the energy transition in the Dominican Republic, where local stakeholders are active subjects in the fight against climate change. Decentralizing the power grid and giving the control of electricity flows to local populations promote empowerment and organization skills among men and women.

Moreover, the process of project implementation together with local communities is an example of how a just energy and people centered transition can be carried out. In fact, the starting point of the project is a specific and expressed need of a local group to solve their access to electricity. The solution to this need comes from a participatory process, where the community and its interests are at the center of the implementation, interacting synergically with other numerous external stakeholders.

Through a learning-by-doing process, community members and organizations train their abilities and acquire new skills. This way, the project turns into a capacity building experience, where people are free to learn and test their knowledge in a protected environment.

2.3 Nonmonetary benefits of social investments in community hydro

Nonmonetary benefits arising from these microhydropower systems are multiple. Most of them are hard to express in terms of monetary value, such as empowerment or capacity building. This difficulty is present even in costs internationally linked to policy, such as the social carbon price, which can range from lows as 25 to highs as 800 dollars per ton [26, 27].

Due to the complexity of interlinked environmental, political, and social systems, quantifying community and environmental benefits is probably not the best strategy to assess the positive impacts and assign a value of return to the social investments in these initiatives. For instance, community microhydropower systems are based on community capitals and the promotion of sustainable livelihoods [28, 29, 30, 31, 32, 33], instead of the promotion of mere financial capital gains or profit.

Following this idea, we can analyze the benefits through quantitative data of environmental and social improvements, as well as qualitative indicators. The scope of this article is not to generate a system of qualitative and quantitative assessment of the impact of community hydropower systems. However, this section will disclose several of the social and environmental benefits that can be used to further build a robust assessment system.

One of the most general benefits from the social investment in community microhydropower is the advancing toward the accomplishment of climate goals and more specifically of working toward a just energy transition. It is also implemented under a perspective of Nature-based Solutions (NbS) that brings together efforts of numerous stakeholders, who make synergy to reach a common objective (Figure 2).

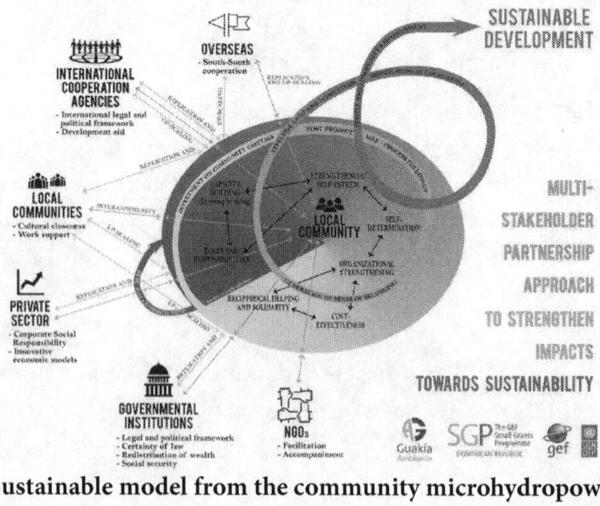

Figure 2. Sustainable model from the community microhydropower systems.

Community microhydro systems contribute to carry out interventions that "protect, sustainably manage, and restore natural and modified ecosystems that address societal challenges effectively and adaptively, simultaneously providing human well-being and biodiversity benefits," aligned to the definition that the International Union for Conservation of Nature (IUCN) provides for NbS [34].

The following Table 1 summarizes the categories and proposes basic initial indicators where community microhydropower systems impact, which can be used as nonmonetary success indicators in terms of social investment:

Table 1. Basic indicators to measure the nonmonetary success of social investment.

Category	Indicators
Decentralized generation from a renewable energy source	• Number of isolated mini-grids implemented. • Number of hydropower turbines installed. • Number of community-based management systems established.
Energy efficiency	• Number of people trained on energy efficiency that implement virtuous behaviors in their communities. • Percentage of households with breakers limiting consumption.
Productive use of energy	• Number of enterprises developed in communities after the installation of a microhydropower system. • Increase in revenue from sustainable tourism. • Decrease in unemployment rate in communities.
Forest conservation and watershed management	• Increase of forested land. • Improvement of water flow. • Improvement of water quality. • Sediment control. • Number of community-based environmental control systems. • Area of ecosystems restored. • Increase in biodiversity.
Capacity building	• Number of Community-Based Organizations (CBOs) that implement effective administration and local finance management. • Number of local technicians, especially young people, trained and working. • Number of people and households that implement environmentally friendly practices.

Category	Indicators
Local empowerment, gender equality, and social inclusion	• Change in time women spend doing chores. • Increase in the number of women dedicating to productive activities. • Increase in the number of women and young people having institutional roles in their communities. • Reduction of migration rate from rural communities. • Number of conflicts solved through participatory mechanisms. • Number of intercommunity networks established and operating.
Socio environmental and economic benefits	• Reduction of household energy expenditure. • Increase in entrepreneurship. • Improvement of productivity. • Development of sustainable livelihoods. • Number of initiatives replicated and/or scaled up. • Statal savings for electricity generation.
Climate change mitigation and adaptation	• $CO2$ emissions avoided. • $CO2$ absorbed. • Number of practices established to protect against extreme events. • Reduction of the impact of extreme events.

Using merely traditional financial indicators, community microhydropower systems might not be the best financial option. However, if we use the previous indicators and, at the same time, we are able to quantify the climate and social benefits, they might as well be profitable. For example, the costs associated with a typical 20-kW system are $300,000, of which around 75% is not refundable if you consider only economic indicators. This means that, if we want to apply a social investment framework, we must build new nonmonetary ways of quantifying returns of investment, which includes the previous indicators.

2.4 A multi-stakeholder approach of sustainability and social investment

In this process, the role of the private sector and its social investments in the community microhydropower systems has been progressively growing in the country and becoming a significant component of the implementation of the projects. Likewise, this interaction among civil society organizations, community members, government officials, and private entities has strengthened the Corporate Social Responsibility policy of several national companies and is becoming central to their social and business agenda.

Among them, the action of the Popular Group (Grupo Popular) stands out. It is one of the main financial groups of the Dominican Republic, which has been increasing its action in these initiatives through the Popular Foundation (Fundación Popular), the entity responsible for its social investment agenda, coming across an effective scheme to contribute to integral interventions, overcoming the limitations of specific projects outside of a strategic framework.

Each community microhydro project is financed through concessional investments, basically different types of nonrefundable investments such as seed capital, grants, and donations. Nevertheless, this has not stopped private investors, such as Grupo Popular, to step in and assign a social investment budget to fuel the energy transition and community development. The framework private firms are using to assess the impact of their investments that are not monetary and rely on the idea of community development and sustainability.

To this day, we can estimate that the total investment made in the implementation of microhydro projects under this scheme exceeds 17 million dollars. The social investment from the private sector is around 5% of it, with a significant increase in its participation during the last 10 years. There is still plenty of opportunity for social investors to increase their participation in these projects.

The participation of the private sector in these projects is an alternative to reduce the risks associated with their implementation. Moreover, multi-stakeholder approaches can fuel a virtuous circle of local development based on social investment and sustainability.

Access to basic services, like electricity, is an essential assumption for development. Nevertheless, sustainability is rather strictly linked to social and environmental processes and dynamics that can be promoted among human groups and their territories. According to this perspective, each project can lighten a path to implement coordinated multi-stakeholder processes, aimed to reach wider sustainability goals.

From this point of view, empowerment of people and local organized groups should become a guiding principle for each of the stakeholders who take part in the process, from private entities to government officials. There should be a common effort to strengthen personal and community self-esteem: during the process, people, individually and as a part of a human group, should internalize that they can reach previously planned goals.

These interventions contribute to educating people to freedom, providing them the opportunity to acquire knowledge and instruments that allow them to make decisions and contribute to the development of the social group they belong to. Confidence, especially inside the community, is a key issue: the intervention should help to overcome the common situation where people show more confidence toward outsiders than toward their peers.

Another important triggering factor is the promotion of solidarity among and within stakeholders. The principle according to which maximizing individual benefit would maximize the collective one has revealed all its limitations, especially when it is applied without a vision of social well-being and sustainability, transcending the idea of only seeking economic benefit. The most successful and sustainable societies are those who adopt synergic strategies and invest in their own development. This includes mechanisms of mutual support, which allow people and communities to overcome individual and collective challenges, generating a sense of belonging to the social group and the environment where they live. Solidarity is a key element to increase the positive impacts of social investments, since it promotes a spiral of continuous improvement.

From this point of view, this model of intervention contributes to improving cost-effectiveness, promoting appropriate distribution of the tasks and available resources, avoiding duplicity, and facilitating the elaboration and implementation of middle- and long-term plans.

2.5 Next steps in social investment in the Dominican Republic

According to the experience gained in multiple projects, the development and social investment models must reintroduce the concept of sustainability along with ethics and nonmonetary objectives and indicators. Community development is a complex and slow process, where empowerment is a key to achieving goals.

Social investment in the country has fulfilled a role of filling in the gap of financing projects on a nonrefundable basis. Most of the projects need nonrefundable investments, since the return of investment, measured only in financial terms, would render most of the projects unfeasible for a traditional financial model. However, if there was a way to incorporate social and environmental positive impacts and sustainable development in the framework of financing decisions of other institutions, it would be possible to expand the impact of social investments.

There is also a need to go further in the models of community microhydropower systems in order to create mechanisms to provide monetary returns in order to diversify the source of social investments. It is also possible to take advantage of the existing network of community microhydropower systems and their current savings networks.

There is the example of the community of Angostura, where the first project was implemented through a combination of social investment, donations by international cooperation, and seed capital. Afterward, the local economy was reshaped, and an ecotourism project was developed, as well as a simple but complete self-managed system of monthly payments to a community fund. With these resources, Angostura was able to participate in covering the costs of an expansion of the microhydropower generation, providing more than 10,000 dollars from its community fund.

3. CONCLUSIONS

The use and abuse of natural resources has become an increasingly critical issue to the human and nonhuman population, impairing the human group's capacity to satisfy its own needs. The multidimensional climate crisis is being fueled not only by the burning of fossil fuels but also by the depletion of ecosystems. This has caused an exponentially growing pressure over the environment through unsustainable investments and projects based on a development model that is incompatible with the natural limits of the resources.

In this context, the expected solution should go through a paradigm shift based on empowerment of people and communities, strengthening of solidarity across sectors and stakeholders and finding creative solutions to social investment opportunities. Communities should acquire means and skills to participate freely, actively, and significatively in decision-making processes of development, at any level.

The evidence coming from the experience of community microhydropower systems points out that the reintroduction of ethics in decision-making is fundamental to reach sustainability. In fact, even though the first step is the development of strategies and policies based on a model that is compatible with the recovery and reposition of natural resources, the effectiveness and durability of its implementation are strictly linked to the commitment of the local population in doing so and the cooperation with other stakeholders, far beyond the regime of consequences that has been established.

Based on well-known technology, these initiatives have become a reference of just energy transition experiences, climate action, and integral watershed management, where local communities, interacting with numerous stakeholders in fair conditions, assume the role of guiding their own development, which includes the monitoring and caring of the natural resources in their territories.

Up until now the social investment by the private sector in these projects has increased, but in absolute terms it is still limited. By increasing the participation of the private sector in these climate solutions, based on synergies among stakeholders, such as government agencies, communities, and international cooperation, there is an opportunity for replicating and upscaling these initiatives. As well, risks associated with funding, timings, governance, government changes, among others, can be significantly reduced.

Nonmonetary assessments such as the ones proposed in this paper are necessary to improve the analysis of the return of the social investments, overcoming the present limits and biases of financial assessments. It is also essential to build a framework around social and environmental indicators in order to build a paradigm shift in climate investment. In this sense, Guakía Ambiente, the Small Grants Programme, and other stakeholders are working to face this challenge.

REFERENCES

1. Brimblecombe P. Air pollution in industrializing England. Journal of the Air Pollution Control Association. 1978;28(2):115-118. DOI: 10.1080/00022470.1978.10470577
2. Allen BG. Empire Forest and the Origins of Environmentalism. Cambridge: Cambridge University Press; 2002
3. Hanlon WW. Coal Smoke and the Costs of the Industrial Revolution. Los Angeles: University of California at Los Angeles (UCLA) and National Bureau of Economic Research (NBER); 2016. Available from: https://economics.yale.edu/sites/default/files/hanlon_coal_and_the_costs_of_the_ir_small.pdf
4. Du Pisani JA. Sustainable development – Historical roots of the concept. Environmental Sciences. 2006;3(2):83-96. DOI: 10.1080/15693430600688831
5. von Carlowitz HC, von Rohr JB. Sylvicultura Oeconomica. Bavarian State Library, Munich; 1713
6. Lloyd WF. Two Lectures on the Checks to Population. London: The University of Oxford; 1832. Available from: https://upload.wikimedia.org/wikipedia/commons/3/34/Two_Lectures_on_the_Checks_to_Population.pdf
7. Malthus TR. An Essay on the Principle of Population. London: J. Johnson; 1798. Available from: http://www.esp.org/books/malthus/population/malthus.pdf
8. Wells HG. A Short History of the World. London: Penguin Books; 1946. Available from: http://www.public-library.uk/ebooks/107/86.pdf
9. Boulding KE. The economics of the coming spaceship earth. In: Jarrett H, editor. Environmental Quality in a Growing Economy. Baltimore: Johns Hopkins University Press; 1966. pp. 3-14
10. Ehrlich PR. The Population Bomb. New York: Buccaneer Books; 1968
11. Toynbee A. Mankind and Mother Earth: A Narrative History of the World. Oxford: Oxford University Press; 1976
12. Lovelock JE. Gaia and the Theory of the Living Planet. Denver, Gaia; 2005

13. Oosthoek J, Gills BK. Humanity at the crossroads: The globalization of the environmental crisis. Globalizations. 2005;2(3):283-291. DOI: 10.1080/14747730500409454

14. United Nations. Transforming our World: The 2030 Agenda for Sustainable Development. New York: United Nations General Assembly, Resolution A_RES_70_1_E; 2015. Available from: https://www.un.org/en/development/desa/population/migration/generalassembly/docs/globalcompact/A_RES_70_1_E.pdf

15. Kheel J. Waking the Sleeping Giant: Unlocking the Hidden Power of Business to Save the Planet. Carson City, Nevada: Lioncrest Publishing; 2021

16. Sánchez A, Izzo M. Micro hydropower: An alternative for climate change mitigation, adaptation and development of marginalized local communities in Hispaniola island. Climatic Change. 2016;140:79-87. DOI: 10.1007/s10584-016-1865-0

17. International Finance Corporation. Strategic Community Investment: A Good Practice Handbook for Companies Doing Business in Emerging Markets. Washington DC: International Finance Corporation; 2010. Available from: https://openknowledge.worldbank.org/handle/10986/27842

18. Office of Investor Education and Advocacy. Environmental, Social and Governance (ESG) Funds – Investor Bulletin [Online]. 2021. Available from: https://www.investor.gov/introduction-investing/general-resources/news-alerts/alerts-bulletins/investor-bulletins-1. [Accessed: June 14, 2022]

19. Gulakov I, Vanclay F, Arts J. Modifying social impact assessment to enhance the effectiveness of company social investment strategies in contributing to local community development. Impact Assessment and Project Appraisal. 2020;38(5):382-396. DOI: 10.1080/14615517.2020.1765302

20. United Nations Global Compact. Principles for Social Investment. The Global Compact. 2010. Available from: https://d306pr3pise04h.cloudfront.net/docs/networks_around_world_doc%2Fcommunication%2F2010-03-08%2FPRSI.pdf

21. United Nations Department of Economic and Social Affairs. World Social Report 2020: Inequality in a Rapidly Changing World. New York: United Nations Department of Social Affairs; 2020. Available from: https://www.un.org/development/desa/dspd/wp-content/uploads/sites/22/2020/02/World-Social-Report2020-FullReport.pdf

22. Intergovernmental Panel on Climate Change. WGII Sixth Assessment Report Chapter 15. IPCC; 2022. Available from: https://www.ipcc.ch/report/ar6/wg2/downloads/report/IPCC_AR6_WGII_FinalDraft_Chapter15.pdf

23. Oficina Nacional de Estadística. Boletín de estadísticas oficiales de pobreza monetaria. Boletín Semestral No. 3. Santo Domingo: Oficina Nacional de Estadísticas; 2016. Available from: https://web.one.gob.do/media/v0hbb1si/bolet%C3%ADn-de-estad%C3%ADsticas-oficiales-de-pobreza-monetaria-no-3.pdf

24. OECD/UNCTAD/ECLAC. OECD Development Pathways, Production Transformation Policy Review of the Dominican Republic: Preserving Growth, Achieving Resilience. Paris: OECD Publishing; 2020. DOI: 10.1787/1201cfea-en

25. Small Grants Programme. Relación de proyectos microhidroeléctricos en ejecución. Santo Domingo: Programa de Pequeños Subsidios y Guakía Ambiente; 2022

26. Ricke K, Drouet L, Caldeira K, et al. Country-level social cost of carbon. Nature Clim Change. 2018;8:895-900. DOI: 10.1038/s41558-018-0282-y

27. Alatorre JE, Caballero K, Ferrer J, Galindo LM. El costo social del carbono: una visión agregada desde América Latina. Santiago: CEPAL; 2018. Available from: https://repositorio.cepal.org/bitstream/handle/11362/44423/1/S1800462_es.pdf

28. Carney D. Approaches to Sustainable Livelihoods for the Rural Poor. Vol. 2. ODI Poverty Briefing, London; 1999

29. Hussein K. Livelihood Approaches Compared: A Multi-Agency Review of Current Practice. London: Commissioned by the UK Department for International Development's (DFID's); Sustainable Livelihoods Support Office (SLSO); 2002

30. Flora CB, Flora JL, Fey S. Rural Communities: Legacy and Change. Oxford: Westview Press; 2004

31. Flora CB. The Community Capitals Framework: A Systemic Approach to Environmental Leadership. Iowa, USA: Annual Community Capitals Framework Institute. Des Moines; 2011

32. Gutiérrez I, Siles J. Diagnóstico de medios de vida y capitales de la comunidad de Humedales de Medio Queso, Los Chiles, Costa Rica. San José, Costa Rica: UICN, Oficina Regional para Mesoamérica y la Iniciativa CARIBE; 2008

33. Gutiérrez-Montes I, Siles J, Bartol P, Imbach AC. Merging a landscape management planning approach with the community capitals framework: Empowering local groups in land management processes in Bocas del Toro, Panama. Community Development. 2009;40(2):220-230. DOI: 10.1080/15575330903004418

34. International Union for Conservation of Nature. About Nature-Based Solutions [Online]. 2022. Available from: https://www.iucn.org/theme/nature-based-solutions/about. [Accessed: June 14, 2022]

CHAPTER 7

KEPT PROMISES? THE EVOLUTION OF THE EU FINANCIAL CONTRIBUTION TO CLIMATE CHANGE

1. INTRODUCTION

The UNFCCC signed a crucial milestone in the international cooperation with the objective, called "the ultimate objective," of achieving "stabilization of greenhouse gas concentrations in the atmosphere at a level that would prevent dangerous anthropogenic interference with climate system" (art. 2 of the Convention[1]) [1] due to the consideration that the climate change calls for the widest possible cooperation by all countries.

The Convention recognizes the need to cooperate and promote a supportive economic system in order to address a path of sustainable economic growth and development of all Parties, particularly developing country Parties. The Convention is based on the fundamental acknowledgment that the climate is a common resource whose stability is threatened by GHG emissions (precautionary principle) and, at the same time, that all countries have all common but differentiated responsibilities and respective capabilities, social and economic conditions in order to protect the climate system for the benefit of present and future generations.

The differentiated commitment between developed and developing countries is the basis for negotiation between the Parties: how, with what means and with what resources. According to the Convention, developed country Parties shall provide financial resources to assist developing country Parties in the implementation of the Convention (art. 11).

It will take until COP15 in 2009 for developed countries to make a collective economic commitment of USD 30 billion for the period 2010–2012 geared toward both mitigation and adaptation, an amount that could rise to USD 100 billion dollars a year by 2020 to address the needs of developing countries. This funding will come from a wide variety of sources, public and private, bilateral and multilateral, including alternative sources of finance (Copenhagen Accord, para. 8) [2].

The Copenhagen Accord is a non-legally binding agreement, but it marks an important turning point. The following year, in fact, during the COP16 in Cancun, the parties confirmed their commitment to the creation of the USD 30 billion fast truck fund by 2012 and then to reach USD 100 billion by 2020, as reported in paragraphs 95 and 98 of the Cancun Agreements, inviting developed country Parties to submit an information document on how the resources would be provided to fulfill the finance commitment [3].

In 2015, the global attention was oriented toward the sustainability and the need to stress the fight against climate change. The role of finance to support climate change has been stressed first with the 2030 Agenda on Sustainable Development Goals (SDGs) [4] and then with the Paris Agreement signed at COP21 [5].

The 2030 Agenda, with its 17 goals and 169 targets, represents a comprehensive and extensive road map for aligning not only developing countries but also developed ones on the path of sustainable development [4], ensuring, simultaneously, human well-being, economic prosperity, and environmental protection. This integrated strategy called "5P" is aimed to promote well-being of the People (p.1); to preserve our natural resources in this Planet (p.2); to eliminate the extreme poverty and to assure Prosperity (p.3) for all, through promotion of Peace (p.4) based on human rights, justice, and rule of law, and through the Partnership (p.5) across nations, sectors, and communities [6, 7]. The 2030 Agenda, in its holistic nature, also focuses on climate change through the SDG 13—*Take urgent action to combat climate change and its impacts.* In particular, its SDG 13.a—"*Implement the commitment undertaken by developed country parties to the UNFCCC to a goal of mobilizing jointly USD 100 billion annually by 2020 from all sources to address the needs of developing countries in the context of meaningful mitigation actions and transparency on implementation and fully operationalize the Green Climate Fund through its capitalization as soon as possible*" reinforces the international commitment remarked also by the Paris Agreement.

In fact, the Paris Agreement provides an ambitious opportunity to consolidate the relationship between climate and development [8, 9], but also to stress the global commitment to mobilize climate finance to support countries, especially LDCs (least developed countries) and developing countries, a worldwide step in strengthening SDG 13.a [8, 10].

To ensure information, transparency, and tracking of the climate finance, the developed country Parties shall use the "UNFCCC biennial reporting guidelines for developed country Parties" for the preparation of the finance reporting [11]. The Biennial Reports (BR) show the progress in meeting their 2020 targets and their provision of financial, technology, and capacity building in supporting to developing country Parties.

According to [12], the total public financial support reported by Annex II Parties amounted to USD 45.4 billion in 2017 and USD 51.8 billion in 2018. In this context, as reported by the Secretariat [13], total climate support reached an annual average of USD 48,7 billion in 2017–2018 (fourth Biennial Report—BR4), which represents a 9.9% increase over the previous biennium 2015–2016 on a comparable basis.

Although the data for 2019–2020 are not yet available, it is known that the target was not reached first because it was too ambitious and second because of the pandemic emergency linked to COVID-19, which distracted and restricted available finance [14, 15].

Climate-specific financial support increased by 13% on a comparable basis, to an annual average of USD 36.3 billion, mainly reported through bilateral, regional, and other channels (USD 28.1 billion in 2017 and USD 31.8 billion in 2018, respectively) [12].

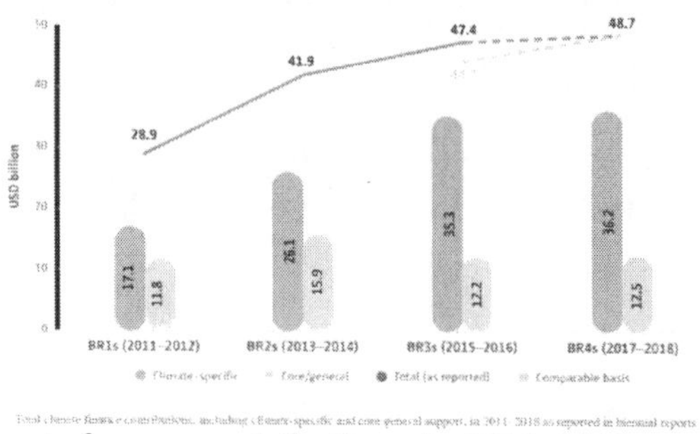

Figure 1. Total climate finance contributions, in 2011–2019 as reported in biennial reports. Source: [13].

The data shown in Figure 1 are realized by the Secretariat on the base of Biennial Report (BR) that collects the public finance data, even if the climate finance should be referred to public, private, and alternative sources of financing. In particular, as required by the Paris Agreement mobilizing climate finance should involve a wide variety of sources.

The chapter aims to illustrate the evolution of the financial commitment of the EUplus, considered as the entire EU with its 28 Member States, including the United Kingdom, through the analysis of the fourth Biennial Report, which covers the period 2011–2018.

2. THE ROLE OF EUROPEAN CLIMATE FINANCE

Like the other Parties to the Convention, the EU Member States have committed themselves to contribute to the fight against climate change not only by reducing their own emissions, but also by supporting developing countries with financial contributions. However, in addition to the commitment of the individual Member States, there is also the contribution directly from the European budget.

The contributions to climate finance, communicated as referred to the Biennial Report (Common Tabular Formats TRF), are classified into:

- ☆ core general: this refers to amounts intended to support multilateral institutions, where, however, it is not possible to identify the specific climate allocation, including contributions to the functioning of the institutions;
- ☆ -specific: refers to amounts earmarked for climate support, which may be linked to adaptation, mitigation, or cross-cutting projects.

According to the relevant international organizations (OECD [16], IPCC [17]), the definitions are:

- ☆ change mitigation is defined as an activity that contributes to the objective of stabilization of greenhouse gas (GHG) concentrations in the atmosphere at a level that would prevent dangerous anthropogenic interference with the climate system by promoting efforts to reduce or limit GHG emissions or to enhance GHG sequestration;
- ☆ change adaptation is defined as an activity that intends to reduce the vulnerability of human or natural systems to the impacts of climate change and climate-related risks, by maintaining or increasing adaptive capacity and resilience.

As shown in Figure 2, the EUplus, as defined above, contribution to the functioning of the institutions (core general) has progressively decreased from just over 47% in 2011–2012 (BR1) to 22% in 2017–2018 (BR4), in favor of a progressive growth of the climate-specific contribution. In truth, if only the EU contribution was considered, almost entirely was for climate, with the only exception is in the 2-year period 2015–2016 (BR3), where, however, the core general was only 0.01%.

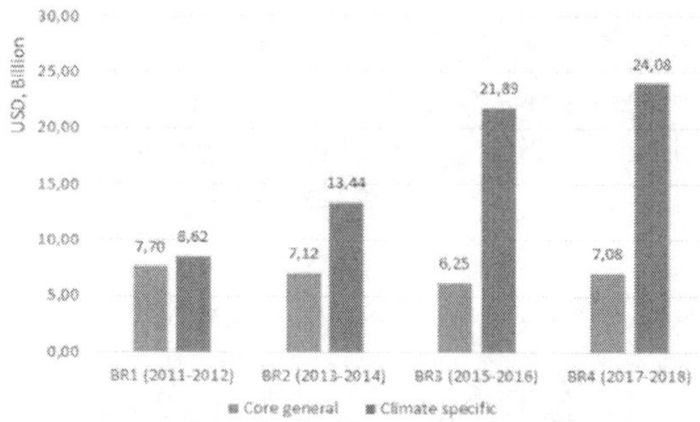

Figure 2. EUplus total public contribution: core general vs. climate-specific. Source: elaboration on [18].

Looking at the types of climate action (Figure 3), investments are mainly oriented toward mitigation, whose amount decreased from 58% in the first 2-year period to 41% in 2017–2018, followed by adaptation, whose amount has remained almost constant over time (around 17–21%), while the relevance of investments classified as cross-cutting increased from 16% in 2011–2012 to 24%.

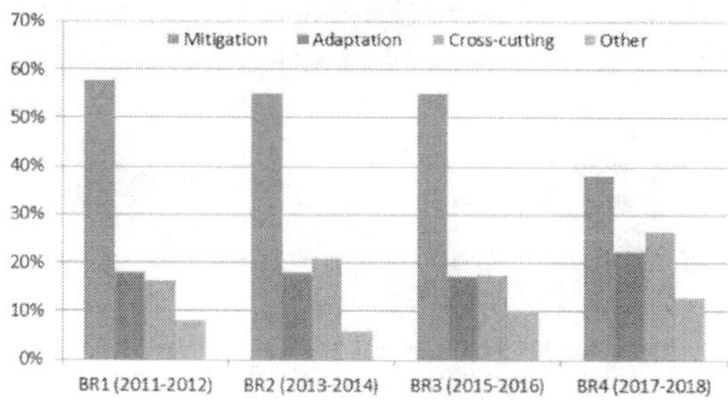

Figure 3. EUplus: climate-specific breakdown in 2011–2018 as reported in biennial reports. Source: elaboration on [18].

Even if the contribution to climate finance could be realized by both multilateral channel and bilateral channel, the amount of the bilateral channel is significantly more relevant, as shown in Figure 4.

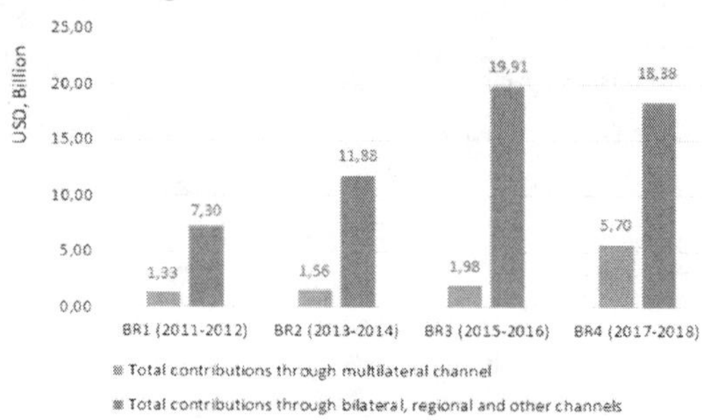

Figure 4. EUplus climate-specific finance: type of channel for contribution in 2011–2018. Source: elaboration on [18].

2.1 Contributions through bilateral channel

With an overall increase in climate-specific contributions of 179% between the 2-year period 2011–2012 and 2017–2018, the percentage becomes more comparable in the 2-year comparison 2015–2016 and 2017–2018 where the increase is 10%.

This is consistent with the allocation of contributions to climate-specific precisely because since 2015 there has been a new and strong drive in the commitment to combat climate change.

The BR analysis shows that EUplus appears to operate predominantly through bilateral channels, which, after peaking at 91% in the 2015–2016, lost ground in the following biennium, dropping to 76%.

In terms of support, bilateral contributions have gradually become more oriented toward mitigation and adaptation. In fact, a comparison of the data reported in the four biennial reports (Figure 5) shows a gradual increase in contributions with a clear attribution of support (mitigation, adaptation, and cross-cutting) while the item "other" becomes residual. At the same time, there is a reorientation of contributions with a greater focus on adaptation than on mitigation.

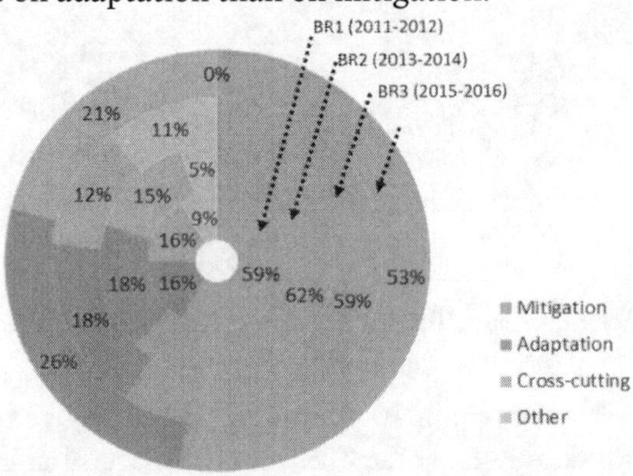

Figure 5. Climate-specific finance of EUplus: bilateral contribution by type of support. Source: Elaboration on [18].

Besides the observation that the focus on adaptation is growing, a detailed analysis per Member States shows that there is a certain homogeneity of orientation, with some exception among most Member States. For example, Denmark, Luxembourg, the Netherlands, Sweden, and the United Kingdom have oriented their contribution toward activities supporting both mitigation and adaptation. In contrast, countries such as Belgium, Estonia, Finland, Ireland, and Spain have favored cross-cutting actions (Table 1).

Table 1. Climate-specific finance of EU and Member States: bilateral contribution by type of support.

	Mitigation	Adaptation	Cross-cutting	Other
EU	↓ 23%	↑ 41%	↓ 36%	–
Austria	↓ 72%	↑ 13%	↑ 14%	–
Belgium	↓ 15%	↓ 56%	↑ 29%	–
Czech Republic	↓ 24%	↑ 65%	↓ 11%	
Denmark	↑ 41%	↑ 22%	↓ 36%	–
Estonia	↓ 13%	↓ 28%	↑ 59%	–
Finland	↓ 28%	↓ 14%	↑ 57%	–
France	↓ 66%	↑ 20%	↓ 13%	–
Germany	62%	↑ 19%	↑ 19%	↓ 0%
Greece	0%	↓ 0%	↑ 100%	–
Hungary	1%	↓ 23%	↑ 76%	–
Ireland	↓ 1%	↓ 28%	↑ 71%	–
Italy	↓ 13%	↑ 24%	↓ 63%	–
Latvia	0%	0%	↑ 100%	–
Luxemburg	27%	↑ 43%	↓ 29%	–
Malta	0%	100%	↓ 0%	–
Netherland	17%	↑ 52%	↓ 31%	–
Poland	↓ 1%	↑ 98%	↓ 1%	–
Portugal	↓ 46%	↑ 54%	↓ 0%	–
Slovakia	44%	↓ 53%	↓ 3%	–
Spain	↓ 81%	↓ 8%	↑ 11%	–
Sweden	22%	↑ 45%	↓ 32%	–
UK	49%	↑ 49%	↓ 0%	↓ 0%

Note: The breakdown for type of support is based on BR4 data, while the arrows show the trend respect to the BR3.

Source: elaboration on [18].

The overall amount of bilateral public climate contribution in 2014 was around 12 BIL USD, mitigation aid accounted for 62%, while adaptation was around 16%. In 2018, the total amount increased at 19 BIL USD with mitigation at 48% and adaptation and cross-cutting at 27% each (Figure 6).

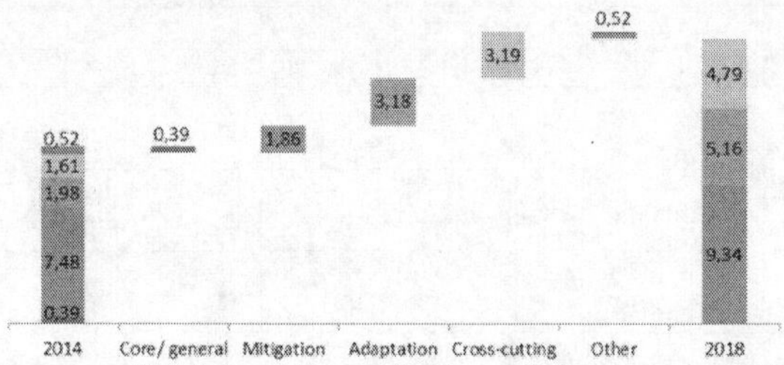

Figure 6. Climate finance of EUplus: the evolution of type support from 2014 to 2018 in bilateral contribution (USD, billion). Source: elaboration on [18].

2.2 Contributions through multilateral channel

The contribution through multilateral channel is composed of three items:

☆ to multilateral climate change funds: the Global Environment Facility; the Least Developed Countries Fund; the Special Climate Change Fund; Adaptation Fund, Green Climate Fund; UNFCCC Trust Fund for Supplementary Activity, and Other multilateral climate change funds;

☆ contribution to multilateral financial institutions, including regional development banks: mainly related to the six major Multilateral Development Banks (MDBs)—World Bank, International Finance Corporation, African Development Bank, Asian Development Bank, European Bank for Reconstruction and Development, and Inter-American Development Bank;

☆ contribution to specialized United Nations bodies.

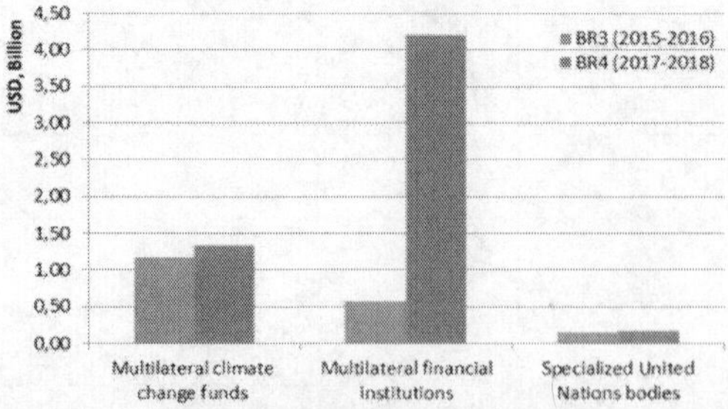

Figure 7. Climate finance of EUplus: multilateral contribution in BR3 vs. BR4. Source: elaboration on [18].

As shown in Figure 7, EUplus contribution to the multilateral channel grew almost three times in the last 2 years compared with the previous 2-year period: 63% are committed contributions and only 37% disbursed contributions. The most relevant part is linked to the multilateral financial institutions, followed by the funds.

A detailed analysis by multilateral channel is given below.

2.2.1 Contribution to multilateral climate change funds

The contribution to multilateral climate change funds constitutes 23% of the contributions under the multilateral channel, mainly provided in cross-cutting activities. As reported in Figure 8, a comparison between 2015–2016 and 2017–2018 shows an increase in "cross-cutting" support, which has essentially replaced the "other" category, followed by an increase in both "mitigation" and "adaptation" support.

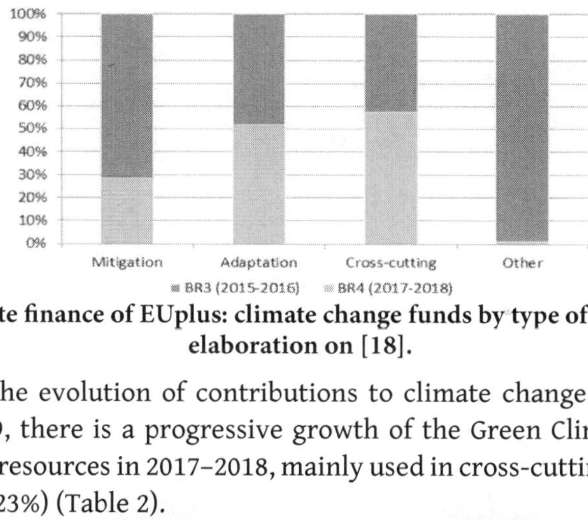

Figure 8. Climate finance of EUplus: climate change funds by type of support. Source: elaboration on [18].

Looking at the evolution of contributions to climate change funds in the last two BR, Figure 9, there is a progressive growth of the Green Climate Fund, which absorbed 68% of resources in 2017–2018, mainly used in cross-cutting activities (77%) and mitigation (23%) (Table 2).

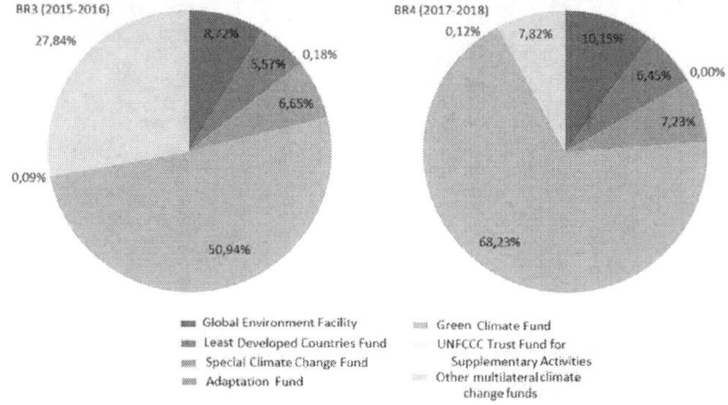

Figure 9. Climate finance of EUplus: multilateral climate change funds (BR3 vs. BR4). Source: elaboration on [18].

Table 2. Multilateral climate change fund: weight and contribution by type of support.

	Mitigation	Adaptation	Cross-cutting	Other
Multilateral Climate Change Fund	↓ 8%	↓ 18%	↑ 74%	↓ 0%
Global Environment Facility	↓ 29%	—	↓ 71%	—
Least Development Countries Fund	—	↓ 95%	↑ 5%	—
Special Climate Change Fund	—	↓ 0%	—	—
Adaptation Fund	—	100%	—	—
Green Climate Fund	—	—	100%	—
UNFCC Trust Fund for Supplementary Activity	↑ 3%	↓ 0%	↑ 97%	—
Other multilateral climate change fund	↓ 53%	↑ 19%	↓ 28%	↓ 0%

Note: The breakdown for type of support is based on BR4 data, while the arrows show the trend respect to the BR3.
Source: elaboration on [18].

2.2.2 Contribution to multilateral financial institutions

The contribution to multilateral financial institutions, including regional development banks, constitutes over 74% of the contributions under the multilateral channel, even for the multilateral financial institutions the support is earmarked to "cross-cutting" activities (Figure 10).

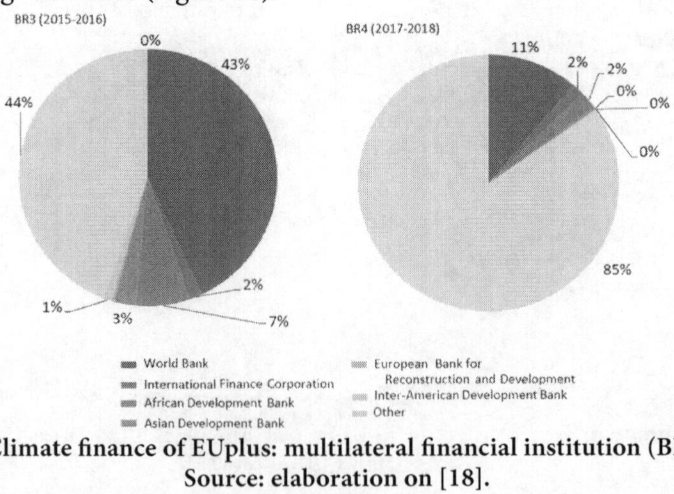

Figure 10. Climate finance of EUplus: multilateral financial institution (BR3 vs. BR4). Source: elaboration on [18].

Looking at the evolution of contributions to financial institutions in the last two BR, there is a progressive decrease of World Bank allocation whose amount passed from 43% to 11%, while the item "other" has increased by both the member fees paid for participation in certain institutions and the participation in projects promoted by regional development banks (e.g., EIB, Latin America Development Bank) or research institutions (e.g., IRENA, IEA, OECD) (Table 3).

Table 3. Multilateral financial institutions: weight and contribution by type of support.

Multilateral financial institutions	↓ 2%	↑ 4%	↓ 94%	↑ 0%
World Bank	—	↓ 0%	↑ 100%	—
International Finance Corporation	↓ 4%	—	↑ 96%	—
African Development Bank	—	—	↑ 100%	—
Asian Development Bank	—	—	↑ 100%	—
European Bank for Reconstruction and Development	↓ 0%	—	↑ 100%	—
Inter-American Development Bank	↓ 0%	—	↑ 100%	—
Other	↓ 2%	↓ 5%	↓ 93%	↑ 0%

Note: The breakdown for type of support is based on BR4 data, while the arrows show the trend respect to the BR3.

Source: elaboration on [18].

2.2.3 Contribution to specialized United Nations bodies

Table 4. Multilateral financial institutions: weight and contribution by type of support.

	Mitigation	Adaptation	Cross-cutting	Other
Specialized United Nations bodies	↓ 7%	↓ 26%	↑ 67%	—
UNDP—United Nations Development Programme	↓ 1%	↑ 15%	↑ 84%	—
UNEP—United Nations Environment Programme	↓ 19%	↑ 35%	↓ 46%	—
Other	↓ 7%	↓ 26%	↑ 67%	—

Note: The breakdown for type of support is based on BR4 data, while the arrows show the trend respect to the BR3.

Source: elaboration on [18]

Finally, in the third multilateral channel relates to the specialized United Nations bodies, the prevailing type of support is "cross-cutting," both because the contributions to the United Nations are collected on sustainability issues (e.g., UNICEF, FAO, IPCC, WMO), and because of the broad structure of the activities in which these bodies operate (Table 4).

3. CONCLUSION

The analysis of Biennial Report data gives the possibility to get a picture of public climate finance mobilized for climate actions from EUplus. Measuring and accounting the financial flows allocated to the action against the climate change. This picture is undoubtedly partial but, however, allows making the point on changing attention of Member States and the EU to climate change.

The analysis of the Biennial Reports showed that since 2015, the push to tackle climate change through financial support in developing countries has gained momentum. The analysis also shows an increasing focus on adaptation-oriented actions, which has thus surpassed contributions to mitigation, a sign of a shift in awareness of the delay we are operating in.

While overall in EUplus mitigation used to absorb 57% of public climate finance, this percentage has dropped to 41% in the last BR in favor of a lower increase in adaptation.

In overall terms, the boost from major international commitments in 2015 led to an increase in EUplus contributions of +63% in 3BR compared with the previous pre-Paris BR (BR2) and + 10% in BR4.

Looking at the type of contribution, the bilateral part constitutes the main item, although in a detailed analysis by individual Member States, the breakdown may not be confirmed.

However, these considerations on the allocation of contributions could be challenged by the BR5 data covering the 2-year period 2019–2020. The new BR will not only give an account of whether or not the global target has been reached, but will also illustrate the impact that the COVID-19 pandemic and the subsequent health emergency have caused both in terms of the volume of investments themselves and in terms of the type of support.

The updated data will be available no later than December 31, 2022 [19], together with the annual greenhouse gas inventory for year 2020 as the first biennial transparency report (BTR1), or at the latest by December 31, 2024, if submitted as a stand-alone report.

At that time we will know whether the promises have been kept or not.

REFERENCES

1. United Nations. General Assembly. United Nations Framework Convention on Climate Change: Text. UNEP/WMO Information Unit on Climate Change, 1992
2. United Nations. Copenhagen Accord, Decision 2/CP.15, Report of the Conference of the Parties on its fifteenth session, held in Copenhagen from 7 to 19 December 2009, FCCC/CP/2009/11/Add.1, 2010
3. United Nations. The Cancun Agreements, Decision 1/CP.16, Report of the Conference of the Parties on its sixteenth session, held in Cancun from 29 November to 10 December 2010, FCCC/CP/2010/7/Add.1, 2011
4. United Nations. General Assembly. Transforming Our World: The 2030 Agenda for Sustainable Development; A/RES/70/1, United Nations, New York, NY, USA, 2015
5. United Nations. Adoption of The Paris Agreements. Report No. FCCC/CP/2015/L.9/Rev.1, 2015
6. Available from: https://www.sdg.services/principles.html [Accessed: May 10, 2022]
7. Barbier EB, Burgess JC. The sustainable development goals and the systems approach to sustainability. Economics. 2017;11:1-23
8. Hwang H, An S, Lee E, Hans S, Lee, C.-h. Cross-societal analysis of climate change awareness and its relation to SDG 13: A knowledge synthesis from text mining. Sustainability. 2021;13:5596
9. Sebestyén V, Domokos E, Abonyi J. Focal points for sustainable development strategies- Text mining-based comparative analysis of voluntary national reviews. Journal of Environmental Management. 2020;263:110414
10. Gomez-Echeverri L. Climate and development: Enhancing impact through stronger linkages in the implementation of the Paris Agreement and the Sustainable Development Goals (SDGs). Philosophical Transaction of Royal Society A. 2018;376:20160444
11. United Nation. Decision 19/CP.18 Common tabular format for "UNFCCC biennial reporting guidelines for developed country Parties", Report FCCC/CP/2012/8/Add.3. 2012
12. United Nation. Summary by the Standing Committee on Finance of the fourth (2020) Biennial Assessment and Overview of Climate Finance Flows UNFCCC Standing Committee on Finance. 2021

13. United Nation [Internet] Compilation and Synthesis Reports of BRs. 2022. Available from: https://unfccc.int/CandS-report-2020#eq-6 [Accessed: May 10, 2022]

14. Iacobuţă GI, Brandi C, Dzebo A, Duron SDE. Aligning climate and sustainable development finance through an SDG lens. The role of development assistance in implementing the Paris Agreement. Global Environmental Change. 2022;74:102509

15. United Nation. Financing for Sustainable Development Report 2021 of the Inter-agency Task Force on Financing for Development United Nations, New York, NY, USA. 2021

16. OECD & Climate Policy Initiative. Climate finance in 2013-14 and the USD 100 billion goal. London, UK. 2015

17. IPCC. In: R.T. Watson and the Core Team, editor. Climate Change 2001: Synthesis Report. A Contribution of Working Groups I, II, III to the Third Assessment Report of the Intergovernmental Panel on Climate Change. Cambridge and New York: Cambridge University Press; 2001. p. 398

18. United Nation Biennial Reports Data Interface [Internet]. 2022. Available from: https://www4.unfccc.int/sites/br-di/Pages/FinancialSupportSummary.aspx [Accessed: May 5, 2022]

19. United Nation. Revision of the UNFCCC reporting guidelines on national communications for Parties included in Annex I to the Convention (decision 6/CP.25) in Report of the Conference of the Parties on its twenty-fifth session, held in Madrid from 2 to 15 December 2019. Report FCCC/CP/2019/13/Add.1. 2019

CHAPTER 8

ROLE OF MOBILE MONEY AND DIGITAL PAYMENTS IN FINANCIAL INCLUSION FOR SUSTAINABLE DEVELOPMENT GOALS IN AFRICA

1. INTRODUCTION

Alleviation of poverty and enhancing opportunities for inclusive economic growth in part demands that the population is financially included to be able to participate in the internet-based new economy. Financial inclusion enables households to undertake transactions required for daily living as well as social protection [1]. Through financial inclusion, economic agents, for example, households, enterprises, and the government, access financial products that improve their well-being and resilience to unforeseen disruptions such as climate change and pandemics (e.g. COVID-19 and Ebola).

It is paradoxical that in a globalized world, more than one-third of its population is excluded from the formal financial system. Nevertheless, evidence suggests that appropriate financial services can help improve household welfare and promote small enterprises. The traditional financial ecosystem is characterized by weaknesses that financially exclude majority of the population. Although mobile money coupled with digital payments can enable the financial inclusion of the financially excluded, empirical evidence demonstrates that small-sized transactions in the conventional setting are associated with high costs, which makes them unfeasible. Mobile money technology in combination with digital payments can permit small-sized transactions at a cost that is affordable by agents. Well-thought-out combinations of digital payments and mobile money technology can potentially reduce the turn-around time for bulky financial transactions [2]. Due to the aforementioned benefits, leaders in low-income countries have embraced mobile money technology and digital payments to overcome financial exclusion to facilitate inclusive economic growth.

Although none of the Sustainable Development Goals (SDGs) of the United Nations Agenda 2030 is dedicated to finance and financial inclusion, this chapter sought to answer the following questions. To what extent can mobile money technology integrated with digital payments enable financial inclusion, which in turn can lead to sustainable development goals? To what extent financial products on mobile money technology and digital payments enhance social inclusion and thereby inclusive-poverty reducing economic growth? What inhibitors stand in the way of mobile money technology and digital payments in realizing financial inclusion to facilitate inclusive economic growth?

This chapter describes how mobile money and digital payments enable financial inclusion. The paper is organized into five sections and unfolds as follows. The next section presents the conceptualization of financial inclusion while the third section describes the relationship between mobile money and digital payments for financial inclusion. Mobile money and digital payments as enablers for the realization of Sustainable Development Goals (SDGs) is the subject matter of the forth section, while the final section concludes.

2. SOCIAL INCLUSION AND FINANCIAL INCLUSION

Social inclusion has been examined by various scholars, including sociologists, historians, economists, psychologists, and natural scientists. Sociology provides a valuable orientation from which to consider social inclusion, because it illuminates how social integration maintains and manages the ways in which people move about and through their socially stratified worlds [3].

On the other hand, financial exclusion is a small but significant component of social exclusion. The latter has been explained as having two broad components, namely economic or structural exclusion (distributional dimension) and social-cultural (relational dimension) [3]. Economic or structural exclusion (distributional dimension) consists of material deprivation and inadequate access to government as well as semi-government provisions ("social rights"). Here the term "Material deprivation" is used to refer to deficiencies in relation to basic needs and material goods, "lifestyle deprivation," problematic debts, and payment arrears. The lack of access to public services demonstrates itself in longer waiting times coupled with financial obstacles to socioeconomic services. The socioeconomic services include but are not limited to banking services, credit, health services, household finance especially helping with household debt acquisition and management; investment advisory services, business development services, business incubation services as well as business mentoring.

Relatedly, the lack of social-cultural inclusion refers to inadequate integration both socially and culturally. Inadequate integration socially connotes failure to participate in the social functioning of a community (including the absence of social support systems). On the other hand, the lack of integration from a cultural perspective means failure to comply with a community's institutions. These institutions represent the rules that govern expected work ethics, social conduct, adherence to the social security system, behaving in socially acceptable ways as well as full participation in the functioning of one's community.

By and large, social inclusion is the process through which all members of society have equitable access to opportunities. Social inclusion policies and institutions seek to promote meaningful participation in society's development by all members by eliminating the barriers that prevent them from full participation. Inhibitors that affect the rate of social inclusion include but are not limited to: diverse interpretation of social inclusion, lack of funds to finance social enterprises development, lack of community enterprises, and a weak social inclusion model [4].

Similarly, financial inclusion is the ability of hitherto excluded individuals as well as firms to access financial products that are appropriate for their needs at an affordable cost. Individuals and firms who are financially excluded cannot smooth their incomes and expenditures, cannot grow their businesses because they cannot access finance that is outside of the firm, and are financially insecure due to failure to accumulate savings. Specifically, improved financial inclusion facilitates the integration of unbanked individuals and firms into the financial ecosystem through the provision of diverse financial services, investment advisory services as well as investment vehicles [5].

Well-functioning financial systems serve a vital purpose by offering savings, payment, credit, and risk management services and thereby contribute to inclusive economic development. Inclusive financial systems are those with a high share of individuals, households as well as enterprises, which have an access to and use services of a financial nature [6]. Financial systems that are well functioning enable firms and individuals to access resources that in turn enable them to meet their needs of a financial nature. These financial needs include but are not limited to the accumulation of retirement savings, human capital accumulation through investment in education, re-tooling and mentoring, insurance against catastrophic expenditures associated with the consumption of medical services, taking advantage of available investment opportunities, and being able to cope with unexpected disruptions. The failure to use the highlighted financial services, in part, leads to rising income inequality coupled with economic growth, which is not inclusive and which leads to rising unemployment.

Social inclusion and financial inclusion are two major development policy agenda in many countries. Financial inclusion is a crucial driver of economic development, and many countries are implementing ambitious strategies to increase their populations' use of financial services, especially digital financial services [7].

3. MOBILE MONEY AND DIGITAL PAYMENTS VERSUS FINANCIAL INCLUSION

Payments refer to the various ways to transfer money. Advances in payment technology influence household choice of payment methods [8]. Consequently, it is instructive to review how switching between payment types affects financial inclusion of households and ultimately, their welfare. On the one hand, mobile money enables users of mobile phones to deposit, withdraw, and transfer money without having a bank account. Mobile money services are provided by telecommunication companies in conjunction with commercial banks through a network of licenses agents. Mobile money services provide various services including but not limited to making deposits into a virtual wallet, which can be used to make payments for purchases, receipt of remittances, person-to-person payments, person-to-government payments, making saving as well as borrowing. Mobile money is available to individuals with bank accounts as well as those without bank accounts. The provision of financial services to those without bank accounts has helped to financially include individuals who previously lacked access to bank services in Africa. Conversely, digital payments allow households to pay digitally instead of via traditional means such as cash or cheque. They include the use of credit cards, credit cards, e-wallets, and mobile phones.

The Digital Revolution, which started in the 1980s and is ongoing, refers to the advancement of technology from analog electronic and mechanical devices to the digital technology available today. The digital revolution has enabled more persons and firms to access the internet, mobile phones as well as other digital services, which are automated and are controlled by the customer of the service, for example, as an "app" on a mobile phone or tablet PC. The interesting question from the perspective of the global agenda is how the digital revolution can enable to attainment of the sustainable development goals? One potential answer is digital financial inclusion. Digital financial inclusion involves the deployment of the cost-saving digital means to reach currently financially excluded and underserved populations with a range of formal financial services suited to their needs that are responsibly delivered at a cost affordable to customers and sustainable for providers. Inclusive digital financial services include online accounts, mobile money services, electronic payments, combinations of insurance and credit as well as FinTech applications that reach individuals and firms, which were hitherto excluded. If digital financial inclusion is provided through a well-regulated ecosystem, it has the potential to enable economic growth and launch countries on to a trajectory to the realization of sustainable development goals [9].

Digital finance and financial inclusion have several benefits to financial services users, digital finance providers, governments, and the economy. The digital finance issues presented by Ozili [10] are relevant for the ongoing debate and country-level projects directed at greater financial inclusion via digital finance in developing and emerging economies. Digital finance and financial inclusion have the potential to work better for individuals, businesses as well as governments.

Although financial inclusion has a central role in efforts toward global economic empowerment, financial inclusion has been deemed the soft side of financial services. This is because it has received limited or no attention from regulatory, policy as well as financial perspective. A major segment of world's population that is economically disadvantaged is either financially excluded or financially underserved [11]. Financial inclusion helps low-income households to get access to basic financial services such as savings, credit, and insurance, improving their financial self-control, thereby promoting economic growth, which is crucial for the realization of development. Therefore, financial services not only foster economic development but also reduce poverty and income inequality. The lack of financial inclusion is a root cause of other social ills in low-income regions of the world, for instance, intergenerational poverty, lack of food security as well as civil unrest. Financial exclusion is an integral part of social exclusion. Therefore, the financially excluded individuals and firms are socially dependent upon their social networks.

4. STATUS OF MOBILE MONEY AND DIGITAL PAYMENTS IN AFRICA

4.1 Basic facts and the African experience

By allowing people to transact in small amounts, digital payments create new opportunities based on micropayments that characterize the majority of the markets where consumers in Africa operate. In these markets, it is common to find cash transactions dominating the market system. The emergence of digital payments appears to have simplified the transaction process under such markets especially given the insecurity of carrying cash in one's wallet that previously attracted the thieving industry to blossom. One comes to the market simply with his/her mobile phone and finds the mobile money agent right in the market for any money withdrawal for market transactions. Financial inclusion in this case goes beyond mere ease of payments to improving financial lives of the populace in Africa. Well-off relatives in town use the same process to send their poor relatives money to afford the basics of life and to make such transactions possible from near their doorsteps. In fact, one can safely argue that the mobile money establishment has a big role in poverty reduction in Africa and hence would act as a gateway to achieving sustainable development goals. Otherwise stated, the effect of mobile money technology extends beyond financial inclusion to poverty reduction as well as risk management, but also consequently to increased productivity.

Mbidde [12] investigated the connection between financial inclusion and the extent of using mobile money services in Uganda. The findings reveal that apart from making use of mobile money services for buying airtime, these electronic wallet services improved financial inclusion whereby 70% of households used mobile money services for cash withdrawals while 60% of households use mobile money services to pay their bills. A positive change is apparent in terms of improved living standards. Notwithstanding the existing challenges, for example, to a layperson who could neither save money earned out of selling a bag of coffee nor communicate easily to a relative in town to help financially in case of an emergency, the mobile money service is a blessing. It should not be forgotten that many local farmers here and in many parts of Africa, after the sale of a big harvest, could keep their money under the bed or somewhere in the banana plantation in a polythene bag. The risks involved in such a practice were enormous, leading to losses and deeper poverty. Financial inclusion, risk management, and poverty reduction are therefore critical consequential outcomes of mobile money services for an African previously ignored by the expensive inaccessible banking services majorly situated in urban centers.

Therefore, it may not be farfetched to argue that for the case of Sub-Saharan Africa, the potential of financial inclusion in aiding the attainment of the Sustainable Development Goals is much alive. A similar view is reiterated by Kuada [13], who, in reference to SDGs 1, 2, 5, and 8, notes in particular that financial inclusion has the potential to accelerate the pace of enterprise development and job creation in African countries and thereby contribute to economic growth and poverty alleviation. Specifically suggested in maximizing the latter benefits are multifaceted policy interventions and strategies, rather than an attempt to extend the outreach of existing financial institutions. The rationale behind these pragmatic solutions is that the current services are fundamentally flawed in terms of appropriateness to the needs and financial capabilities of the unbanked segments of the population especially in the rural areas of Africa where the majority of the populace can be traced. It is therefore recommended that a multipronged approach should include interventions that strengthen the poorest individuals' control over their experienced situations as well as beliefs in their personal efficacy to take initiatives that will take them out of poverty. Such endeavors would most likely produce long-lasting benefits of financial inclusion to those that have for long been financially excluded involuntarily in Africa. Yet the contribution of the latter to the region's food basket is notably significant.

4.2 Effect of mobile money and digital payments in Africa

The potential of financial inclusion in aiding the attainment of the Sustainable Development Goals in Sub-Saharan African countries has been discussed by various scholars. For instance, Kuada [6] highlights the direct contributions of financial inclusion to the attainment of SDGs 1, 2, 5, and 8. He notes that financial inclusion will accelerate the pace of enterprise development and job creation in African countries and thereby contribute to economic growth and poverty alleviation. Additionally, some of the challenges that need to be rectified have been highlighted. A multipronged approach relating to interventions and strategies is preferred rather than one that seeks to scale up the outreach of existing players in the financial ecosystem. This is because existing services are inappropriate with regard to financial ability as well as needs of the segments of the population that lack access to banking services. Therefore, the multipronged approach should include interventions that strengthen the poorest individuals' control over their experienced situations as well as beliefs in their personal efficacy to take initiatives that will take them out of poverty.

There is also a growing body of empirical literature that documents the potential development benefits of financial inclusion, especially from the use of digital financial services, including mobile money services, payment cards, and other financial technology applications [14]. Mobile money services have been found to permit individuals and firms to store value and transfer value or money by means of a mobile phone. This has in turn aided improvements in people's ability to earn income and thereby reduce poverty. Access to mobile money services among women-headed households in Kenya has been found to access increased savings by at least 20% and reduced extreme poverty by 22%.

Fourth industrial revolution advances in technology have greatly changed the digital payments' ecosystem through among other things: the internet of things, application programming interfaces, biometric technologies, digital identification, cloud computing, and quick response codes. These technologies facilitate new access modes and products [15]. The new products include but are not limited to central bank digital currencies (CBDCs) and stablecoins. Central bank digital currency (CBDC) is money that a central bank can produce. It is called digital (or electronic) because it is not physical money like notes and coins. It is in the form of an amount on a computer or similar device. On the hand, a stablecoin is a digital currency that is pegged to a "stable" reserve asset like the US dollar or gold. Stablecoins are designed to reduce volatility relative to unpegged cryptocurrencies like Bitcoin.

Smallholders with farms under two hectares produce between 70 and 80% of the world's food. Agricultural digital financial services (agri DFS) powered by mobile money can connect smallholder farmers to both local and international markets. Through digitized payments, agricultural digital financial services enable smallholder farmers to receive payments from agribusinesses [16]. Vital transactional data as well as digital footprints enable financial institutions to assess the creditworthiness of smallholder farmers. Nevertheless, the extent to which agricultural value chains are digitized is dependent on the effectiveness of the partnerships and collaboration between cooperatives and agribusinesses on the one hand and mobile money providers as well as other agricultural digital financial services, on the other.

Several studies have been undertaken to estimate the effects of financial inclusion on welfare in Sub-Saharan Africa. These include but are not limited to Ofori-Abebrese et al. [15], who reveal that financial inclusion is low with approximately 88% of sampled countries having a low financial inclusion index. Financial inclusion was found to improve welfare by working through education and income. The positive effect of financial inclusion on welfare has important implications for policy.

Mobile money and digital payments have proved vital during disruptions. When the COVID-19 pandemic emerged, mobile money kept people connected through the delivery of vital financial support as well as providing safe, contactless payment methods for food, electricity, and other essentials of life. Mobile money is a crucial component of daily routine for many people around the world. As at the end of 2021, more US$ billion was transacted each day [17].

In Africa, independent bodies have recently established digital platforms to facilitate the aforementioned transaction processes. For example, *AfricaNenda*, an independent Africa-led coalition of dedicated payment experts, governments, and the private sector launched a digital platform aimed at supporting poor households and creating prosperity opportunities for the underserved population. The coalition aims at accelerating the growth of inclusive payment systems geared toward benefiting all Africans, including those who are economically challenged and are financially excluded.

Digital payments systems have been found to enable the upscaling of government-to-persons social assistance programs. This is because of their affordable cost with regard to reaching persons in hard-to-reach remote locations. Ideally, a social protection program operated through a digitized ecosystem seeking to promote the economic empowerment of women should possess the following desirable attributes: accountable, flexible, accessible, reliable, and secure. Although myriad merits are associated with digitized government-to-persons systems, especially during disruptions such as earthquakes and pandemics, the potential reach is dependent on the available infrastructure to provide digital payments, digital financial services being offered as well as their regulatory framework [15]. Digitized payments ecosystems have reduced the exclusion of women through the provision of access to money in close proximity to where they live and work besides enabling them to receive money in various accounts. Morocco provides an example of a country where advanced government-to-persons fast digital payments have enabled payments to reach those in remote areas by relying on retail agent networks.

Whilst the year 2020 was a year of unexpected and sweeping change, the challenges and strategies were different, but the focus remains the same: an inclusive digital future for all. At the global level, the live services stood at 310 decomposed as follows: Sub-Saharan Africa (157); East Asia and Pacific (49); Europe and Central Asia (9); Latin America and the Caribbean (30); Middle East and North Africa (29); and South Asia (36). The number of registered accounts stood at 1.2 billion decomposed as follows: Sub-Saharan Africa (548 million); East Asia and Pacific (243 million); Europe and Central Asia (21 million); Latin America and the Caribbean (39 million); Middle East and North Africa (56 million); and South Asia (305 million). The number of active accounts stood at 300 million decomposed as follows: Sub-Saharan Africa (159); East Asia and Pacific (52 million); Europe and Central Asia (4 million); Latin America and the Caribbean (16 million); Middle East and North Africa (3 million); and South Asia (66 million). The transaction volume at the global level stood at 41.4 billion decomposed as follows: Sub-Saharan Africa (27.4 billion); East Asia and Pacific (5.4 billion); Europe and Central Asia (234 million); Latin America and the Caribbean (701 million); Middle East and North Africa (146 million); and South Asia (7.5 billion). The transaction value in US$ at the global level stood at 767 billion decomposed as follows: Sub-Saharan Africa (490 billion); East Asia and Pacific (111 billion); Europe and Central Asia (4.0 billion); Latin America and the Caribbean (19.8 billion); Middle East and North Africa (10.5 billion); and South Asia (131 billion) [15].

The number of live services stood at 171 decomposed as follows: West Africa (70); Southern Africa (14); North Africa (14); Central Africa (16); and East Africa (57). Sub-Saharan Africa compared with other regions accounts for much of the growth with respect to mobile money technology. The number of registered mobile money users is more than half a billion. Forty-three percent of all new mobile money accounts are in the region. The registered accounts stood at 562 million (representing 12%

point increase) decomposed as follows: West Africa (198 million); Southern Africa (11 million); North Africa (14 million); Central Africa (46 million); and East Africa (293 million). The number of active accounts stood at 161 million (representing an 18% rise) decomposed as follows: West Africa (47 million); Southern Africa (3 million); North Africa (1 million); Central Africa (16 million); and East Africa (94 million). The transaction volume stood at 27.5 billion (representing a 15% rise) decomposed as follows: West Africa (6.4 billion); Southern Africa (284 million); North Africa (77 million); Central Africa (2.2 billion); and East Africa (18.6 billion). Transaction value (US$) stood at 495 billion (representing a 23% rise) decomposed as follows: West Africa (178 billion); Southern Africa (3.0 billion); North Africa (5.4 billion); Central Africa (35.7 billion); and East Africa (273 billion). Although absolute growth was highest in West and East Africa, Southern Africa grew the fastest at 24% year-on-year [18].

Coulibaly [15] attempted to understand the factors driving the adoption and the use of mobile financial services in the West African Economic and Monetary Union (WAEMU compared with East Africa. Probit and multinomial logit estimations are undertaken using data drawn from the 2017 Global Financial Inclusion database. The same set of determinants drive the adoption and use of mobile money in both groups of countries. Compared with East Africa, the slow uptake of mobile money in WAEMU countries is due to insufficient policies toward raising awareness to the benefits of using mobile financial services. Government officials in WAEMU countries are advised to boost the use of mobile money services by enhancing income levels, introducing incentives to reward higher levels of education attainment.

In some cases, mobile money providers offer bulk payments besides providing agricultural value chain payments to farmers. Overall, as at the end of 2020, 39% of mobile money providers that offered bulk payments also provided agricultural value chain payments to farmers. As at the end of 2021, 120 agricultural organizations around the world used mobile money to digitize value chain payments [14]. Seventy-five percent of these organizations are in Sub-Saharan Africa. Due to the ongoing COVID-19 pandemic, there is growing urgency of financing needs of smallholder farmers. Therefore, agribusinesses are using digital technology to improve their operations to scale up the access of smallholder farmers to financial services. Besides the need for collaboration with specialized technology providers, for instance, *agritech* and *insurtech* companies, there are opportunities for synergy between mobile money providers and agribusinesses to grow their partnerships to serve farmers better. In turn, this will enable them to develop specialized services for the agricultural sector over and above digital payments. This will enable new uses ranging from digital farm as well as farmer records to agricultural insurance, credit, and loan products.

5. CONCLUSION

Financial inclusion has been presented in some global policy documents, for instance, the Universal Financial Access 2020, to be a tool that can potentially reduce socioeconomic deprivation around the world. Financial inclusion of economically challenged households will enable them to accumulate human capital through, for instance, education, consumption of healthcare services, medical insurance, and other social determinants of health.

Mobile money services in conjunction with digital payments have the potential to improve the financial inclusion index across many countries in Sub-Saharan Africa especially those in hard-to-reach remote locations. By improving the financial inclusion of individuals and firms, mobile money services, and digital payments will improve upon their social inclusion, thereby aiding the realization of the sustainable development goals.

Financial technology's benefits for financial inclusion need to address the associated risks [15]. Some of these risks include: (i) development of financial technology requires increased coordination across borders and currencies. Effective coordination among policymakers, regulators, central banks, and supervisors can avert regulatory arbitrage as well as enhance effective supervision and oversight; (ii) there is need to constantly keep abreast of innovations by authorities to mitigate potential regulatory failure and challenges in the application of new business models; and (iii) developments in financial technology have indicated the challenges as well as opportunities associated with extending the access of payment service providers to payments infrastructures as well as the need to guard against cyber-attacks.

The mobile money industry has embraced disruption and built resilience over the COVID-19 pandemic era. The solutions that emerged as well as the growth that occurred despite the pandemic demonstrate evidence of the industry's strong partnerships. These relationships enabled mobile money providers to move quickly, sustain their operations, and contribute to more robust local economies and communities.

The ongoing COVID-19 pandemic catalyzed the realization of changes to the regulatory environment. For instance, the pandemic prompted the simplification as well as streamlining of processes required to sign up for a mobile money account. There is need for regulators as well as governments to constantly consult with industry players in order to create a conducive environment that benefits the long-term sustainability of the industry and benefits consumers [15]. It remains to be seen if the COVID-19 pandemic will affect the use of cash, consumer behavior as well as digitization. As the global economy recovers, the mobile money ecosystem will change the modern economics of mobile money.

While this chapter has focused on the mobile money and digital payments dimension of financial inclusion, fintech firms have enabled the saving as well as the borrowing dimension of financial inclusion. The latter could be an area for future research.

REFERENCES

1. International Financial Corporation. Toward Universal Access: Addressing the Global Challenge of Financial Inclusion. Washington, DC: International Finance Corporation; 2011. © International Finance Corporation. Available from: https://openknowledge.worldbank.org/handle/10986/21742. License: CC BY-NC-ND 3.0 IGO
2. Sapovadia V. Chapter 14 – Financial inclusion, digital currency, and mobile technology. Handbook of Block chain, Digital Finance, and Inclusion. 2018;2:361-385
3. Yawe BL, Prabhu J. Innovation and financial inclusion: A review of the literature. Journal of Payments Strategy & Systems. 2015;9(2):215-228
4. Ozili PK. Social inclusion and financial inclusion: International evidence. International Journal of Development Issues. 2020;19(2):169-186. DOI: 10-1108_IJDI-07-2019-0122
5. Qamruzzaman M, Wei J. Financial innovation and financial inclusion Nexus in South Asian Countries: Evidence from symmetric and asymmetric panel investigation. International Journal of Financial Studies. 2019;7:61. DOI: 10.3390/ijfs7040061
6. World Bank. Financial inclusion. Europe and Central Asia Economic Update. Washington, DC: World Bank Group; 2019
7. Center for Global Development. Building Digital Financial Inclusion: A Decision Tree Approach, CGD Brief. 2021. Available from: https://www.cgdev.org/sites/default/files/Brief-Decision_Tree_FINAL.pdf. [Accessed: April 22, 2022]
8. Agarwal S, Chua YW. FinTech and household finance: A review of the empirical literature. China Finance Review International. 2020;10(4):361-376
9. United Nations. Igniting SDG Progress Through Digital Financial Inclusion. 2018. https://sdgs.un.org/sites/default/files/publications/2655SDG_Compendium_Digital_Financial_Inclusion_September_2018.pdf. [Accessed: April 22, 2022]
10. Ozili PK. Impact of digital finance on financial inclusion and stability. Borsa Istanbul Review. 2018;18(4):329-340

11. Salampasis D, Mention A. Chapter 18 –FinTech: Harnessing Innovation for Financial Inclusion. In: Handbook of Block chain, Digital Finance, and Inclusion. Vol. 2. 2018. pp. 451-461

12. Mbidde J. Mobile Money Services and Financial Inclusion in Rural Areas of Uganda: A Case Study of Bukomansimbi. Kampala, Uganda: Makerere University; 2017

13. Kuada J. Financial inclusion and the sustainable development goals. In: Makina D, editor. Extending Financial Inclusion in Africa. London: Elsevier Inc.; 2019. pp. 259-277. DOI: 10.1016/B978-0-12-814164-9.00012-8

14. Bank for International Settlements. Payments Aspects of Financial Inclusion in the Fintech Era. Washington, DC: World Bank Group; 2020

15. GSM Association. State of the Industry Report on Mobile Money 2021. 2021

16. Ofori-Abebrese G, Baidoo ST, Essiam E. Estimating the effects of financial inclusion on welfare in sub-Saharan Africa. Cogent Business & Management. 2020;7(1):1839164. DOI: 10.1080/23311975.2020.1839164

17. Zimmerman JM, May M, Kellison E, Klugman J. Digital Cash Transfers in Times of COVID-19: Opportunities and Considerations for Women's Inclusion and Empowerment (English). Washington, D.C.: World Bank Group; 2020

18. Coulibaly SS. A study of the factors affecting mobile money penetration rates in the West African Economic and Monetary Union (WAEMU) compared with East Africa. Financial Innovation. 2021;7:25

CHAPTER 9

THE INNOVATION OF SIX-DIMENSIONAL POOLING RISK FRAMEWORK IN UNIVERSAL HEALTH INSURANCE COVERAGE

1. INTRODUCTION

United Nations formulated transformational Sustainable Development Goals (SDGs) vision to transform our world to be free of poverty and disease by 2030 [1], and WHO invented the UHC framework to be a glocalization model to achieve health-related SDGs [2]. The existing outcomes of health-related SDGs in World Health Statistics showed that life expectancy at birth improved 5.5 years globally from 66.5 to 72.0 years between 2000 and 2016 [3]. Life expectancy was 62.7 years in low-income countries and 80.8 years in high-income countries, so it was 18.1 years low in low-income countries in 2016 [3]. Life expectancy progress in low-income countries between 2000 and 2016 was 21%, compared with 8% globally and 4% in high- income countries [3]. Premature deaths in low-income countries were caused by lower respiratory infections, diarrhea diseases, acquired immunodeficiency syndrome (AIDS), malaria, and preterm birth complications [3]. The top three causes of premature death in other countries occurred due to ischemic heart disease, lung cancer, and suicides [3].

Globally in 2015 [4], the figure of maternal deaths was 216 per 100,000 live births. This means the complications of pregnancy and childbirth killed almost 830 women every single day [4]. Poor women in remote areas suffer lack of adequate health care [4]. However, these deaths happened in low-resource settings [4] and could be prevented. The two-thirds of global maternal deaths happened generally in the WHO African Region [4]. The possibility of a 15-year-old girl in the region ultimately dying from a maternal reason remained as high as 1 in 37 compared with 1 in 3400 in the WHO European Region [4]. The maternal deaths occur mainly due to hemorrhage, hypertension during pregnancy, infections, and indirect causes and interaction between preexisting medical conditions and pregnancy [4].

The reduction of the global under-five mortality rate has been reduced from 93 per 1000 live births in 1990 to 41 per 1000 live births in 2016 [5]. Nevertheless in 2016, 15,000 children died before reaching their fifth birthday [5]. In 2016, the majority of 2.6 million newborn deaths occurred in the first week of life [5]. Three-quarters of all neonatal deaths occurred due to prematurity, intrapartum-associated events such as birth asphyxia and birth trauma, and neonatal sepsis [5]. In 2016, the leading causes of death in children aged 1–59 months were acute respiratory infections, diarrhea, and malaria. Older children (aged 5–14 years) died from preventable causes [5].

The causes of death in children under-5 years of age in 2016 were "prematurity, acute respiratory infections, birth asphyxia and birth trauma, tetanus, HIV/AIDS, measles, meningitis/encephalitis, other noncommunicable diseases, malaria, injuries, neonatal sepsis, diarrhea, congenital anomalies, other communicable, perinatal and nutritional conditions" [5]. In 2017, three-quarters (22%) of 151 million stunted (too short for their age) children under the age of 5 live in the WHO South-East Asia Region or WHO African Region [5]. High levels of stunting associated with childhood morbidity and mortality risks, learning capacity, and NCDs later in life have a negative impact on the development of countries [5]. In 2017, the overweight (too heavy for their height) children under the age of 5 were 38 million (5.6%), and the wasted (too light for their height) were 51 million (7.5%) [5].

In 2016, noncommunicable diseases caused 41 million deaths, which were 71% of all deaths worldwide [3]. Most of those deaths occurred from cardiovascular diseases, cancer, chronic respiratory diseases, and diabetes mellitus [3]. The risk factors of noncommunicable diseases include unhealthy diets, insufficient physical activity, raised blood pressure, tobacco use, harmful use of alcohol, obesity, overweight among children, and air pollution [3].

The desired outcomes of health-related SDGs were identified for designing the functions of the universal health insurance coverage. United Nations formulated

SDGs 1, 2, 3, 6, and 10 to transform our world to be free of poverty and diseases by 2030 [1]. The SDGs 1, 2, 3, 6, and 10 consist of ending poverty in all its forms everywhere, generating healthy lives and promoting well-being for all at all ages, ending hunger, achieving food security, improving nutrition, and promoting sustainable agriculture, ensuring availability and sustainable management of water and sanitation for all, and reducing inequality within and among countries [1, 6].

SDG's targets are to reduce global maternal mortality, end preventable deaths of newborns and children under-5 years of age, to end the epidemics of communicable diseases through the three levels of prevention, to reduce premature mortality from communicable and noncommunicable diseases through health promotion and three levels of prevention promote mental health and well-being, strengthen health promotion and treatment of substance abuse (including narcotic drug abuse and harmful use of alcohol), reduce global deaths and injuries from road traffic accidents, ensure universal access to sexual and reproductive healthcare services (including family planning, information and education, and the integration of reproductive health into national strategies and programs), achieve universal health coverage (UHC), including financial risk protection, access to quality essential healthcare services and access to safe, effective, affordable and quality essential medicines and vaccines for all, reduce the number of deaths and illnesses from hazardous chemicals and air, water, and soil pollution and contamination, strengthen the implementation of the World Health Organization Framework Convention on Tobacco Control in all countries (as appropriate), ensure equal opportunity and reduce inequalities of outcome, achieve substantial coverage of the poor and vulnerable by implementing national appropriate social protection systems [1, 6].

The strategic health goals are to reduce inequality within and among countries through equal opportunity by reducing outcome inequalities [1, 6], to achieve healthy lives and promote well-being for all at all ages through health promotion and the higher levels of disease prevention, and to end poverty in all its forms everywhere through universal health insurance coverage [1, 6].

The UHC framework was introduced to ensure everyone has equity in accessibility to promotion, prevention, treatment, and rehabilitation healthcare services, without suffering financial hardship by paying for them [2, 7, 8]. The UHC framework is built around three-dimension components [8]. The components contain universal healthcare services coverage, universal financial risk protection and population coverage with a proportion of the costs covered (Figure 1) [2, 7, 8]. The elements are considered in UHC such as the population covered, the services package, cost sharing for pooling, cost payment for services, and the cost pay by pooling [2, 7, 8].

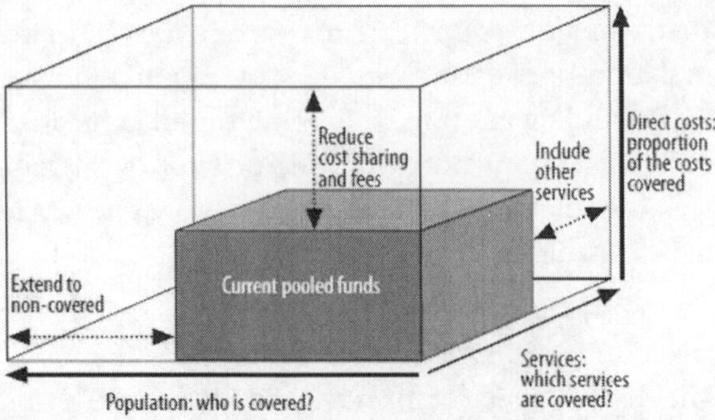

Figure 1. Three dimensions to consider when moving toward universal coverage. Source: the world health report: health systems financing: the path to universal coverage. 2010.

The six functions of the universal health insurance coverage–Bismarck Model were formulated based on SDG 1,2,3,6 and 10 targets. The overarching goal of these functions transforms the determinants of health-related SDGs to produce healthier populations by 2030. Firstly, they protect an insured population from financial risk to reduce out of pocket eradication of poverty in all its forms everywhere. Secondly, they promote health to ensure healthy lives and promote well-being for all at all ages. Thirdly, they prevent diseases to end the epidemics of communicable diseases through the three levels of disease prevention. Fourthly, they finance leaving no district behind universal healthcare services coverage. Fifthly, they finance health promotion, disease prevention, treatment, and palliative services, to transform ecological social determinants of health, to decrease morbidity and mortality rate of communicable diseases and noncommunicable diseases. Finally, they function to ensure equity in access to four types of healthcare services, for leaving no one behind. The Bismarckian model is a sickness fund approach and a state social insurance based on prepayment by employees and their employers [9].

The functional problems of the universal health insurance coverage-Bismarck Model program originated from the lack of health promotion, disease prevention, and reduction of health inequity funds. Those problems make the program ineffective in reducing the morbidity and mortality rate of communicable and noncommunicable diseases and inequity in healthcare service accessibility. This study aims to transform the three-dimension pooling risk framework of the universal health insurance coverage-Bismarck Model to finance healthy lives and equity in healthcare services accessibility.

2. METHODS

A case study design was used to synthesize health insurance-Bismarck model with Sustainable Development Goals (SDGs) 1,2,3,6 and 10, UHC frameworks, the four types of preventions, the district division administrative disaggregation data framework, the district health system, and social determinants of health, to innovate the six-dimension pooling risk framework. In addition, the Precede-Proceed Planning Model was applied to formulate the six-dimension pooling risk framework.

2.1 The precede-proceed planning model

The Precede-Proceed Planning Model embodies assessment, planning, implementation, and evaluation interventions [10]. The Precede part includes phases that are the social assessment, epidemiological assessment, educational and ecological assessment, administrative and policy assessment, and intervention alignment [10]. The Proceed part consists of implementation, process evaluation, impact evaluation, and outcome evaluation [10]. The social assessment aims to identify the quality-of-life issues and to formulate the quality-of-life goals of a community [10]. Then, epidemiological assessment comprises epidemiological, behavioral, and environmental assessment [10]. Epidemiological assessment seeks to create measurable objectives related to the health quality of life outcomes. Behavioral assessment plans to transform behaviors that influence the health outcomes to sub-objectives. Environmental assessment plans to transform physical, social, culture, political, and family environments that influence the health outcomes to sub-objectives [10]. Next, educational and ecological assessments plan to figure out hypothesized mediators of the behaviors identified [10]. They are classified to predisposing factors, reinforcing factors, and enabling factors, and they seek to develop sub-objectives [10]. After that, administrative and policy assessment and intervention alignment seek to evaluate the capacity and resources available to implement programs and transform policies based on the assessed needs [10].

2.2 The types of prevention

The types of prevention are categorized to health promotion, primary, secondary, and tertiary prevention [11]. Health promotion "enables people to increase control over their own health. It covers a wide range of social and environmental interventions that are designed to benefit and protect individual people's health and quality of life by addressing and preventing the root causes of ill health, not just focusing on treatment and cure [12]." Primary prevention is to prevent disease and injury from occurring in the individual and the community [11]. Secondary prevention is to make early diagnosis and promote treatment of a disease or injury stopping the progress or shortening the duration and preventing the complications from the present disease process [11]. Tertiary prevention aims to prevent the severity and the complications of the disease [11].

2.3 The district health system

The UHC framework of Thailand depends on the district health system to accomplish equity to access healthcare services [13]. It has been developed throughout the nation. A district hospital services a population of about 50,000 people, and it consists of 30–120 beds and 100–300 staff. Its staff comprises general doctors, nurses, dentists, pharmacists, and other professionals [13]. The district health system is covered by 10–15 subdistrict health centers [13]. The UHC framework of Thailand reforms strengthened primary care throughout, providing local primary care networks greater management of financial resources, and being "close to the home, close to the heart" community facilities [14]. The Thai framework integrates medical and public healthcare services, so the system provides health promotion, disease prevention, and treatment healthcare services [14]. The UHC framework in 2001, "the district health networks received capitation-based funding for their population that covered services provided within the network and also the costs of referral to secondary care" [14]. Therefore, the local managers are empowered [14]. Health and social services are integrated in Thai district health system to encourage participation of all sectors to cooperate to enhance their local people's quality of life [15].

2.4 The district division administrative disaggregation data framework

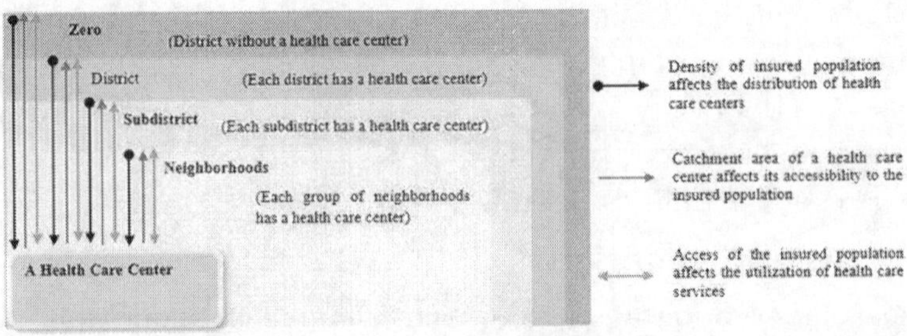

Figure 2. The district division administrative catchment area disaggregation of data framework. Source: district division administrative disaggregation data framework.

The District Division Administrative Disaggregation of Data (DDADD) framework figured out the effect of the density of the insured population in the catchment area distribution of healthcare centers to detect districts left behind [16] (Figure 2). It determined the effect the density of the insured population had on the catchment areas cost of healthcare services (Figure 2) [16]. It found out the effect of the catchment areas distribution of healthcare centers on income-insured accessibility, to identify who is left behind (Figure 2) [16]. It discovered the effect of income-insured catchment area accessibility on the income-insured utilization of healthcare services to identify who was left behind [16]. The DDADD framework identified the insured poor were protected by the equitable distribution of healthcare services in high-density insured population districts [16]. However, the insured poor were left behind by the inequitable distribution in low-density insured population districts [16]. It found out the majority of the population living in low-density population districts were insured poor, and these districts lacked healthcare facilities with high cost of healthcare services [16]. It concluded that low-density-population districts determine health equity outcomes.

The DDADD suggests a premium equation of health insurance scheme that requires transformation based on equity and the probability of illness [16]. This transformation functions to mobilize healthcare resources toward low-density-population districts. Thus, subsidization is needed from the insured population living in high-density-population districts, to those who live in low-density-population districts.

2.5 The existing three-dimension pooling risk framework

The Bismarckian model is a sickness fund approach, and it is state social insurance based on prepayment by workers and their employers [9]. The insured worker utilizes the healthcare services and the state social insurance provides payment to healthcare providers such as physicians, hospitals, or other providers [9]. The framework is organized by prepayment that means participants pay before they are ill, then they depend on the pooled funds from the health insurance scheme when they fall sick [17]. In many health financing systems, prepayment is combined with cost sharing from participants to service providers, and cost sharing is the direct payment [17]. The cost sharing means that the health insurance scheme does not cover all healthcare services costs and the insured person still has to pay a percentage of his or her costs out of pocket [17].

The three-dimension pooling risk framework of the health insurance–Bismarck model aims to accumulate and to manage the financial resources, ensuring that the financial payment risk for health care is carried by all participants of the pool and not by the individuals who become sick [17]. The prepayment is formulated by a large number of people, with pooling of funds to cover everyone's healthcare costs [17]. The framework spreads the financial risk related with the need to use health services [17, 18]. The existing cross-subsidization of the framework composes of the rich subsidizing the poor [19, 20], the healthy subsidizing the sick [19, 20], and the young subsidizing the elderly [17, 20]. Evidence shows the good-quality design and implementation of a subsidization framework have contributed to financial protection, decreasing inequities in access to healthcare services among different income groups, and utilization improvement for the subsidized [21].

The equitable financial mechanism collects the contributions of the health insurance-Bismarck model based on progression, which means higher-income people pay progressively higher proportions of their revenue [22]. In low- and middle-income countries, health insurance is a sustainable healthcare financing model for offering financial risk protection for the majority of the population [23]. In Germany, Statutory Health Insurance has been compulsory for all citizens and the premium for permanent residents is a uniform contribution of 15.5% of their revenue with 118 sickness funds in 2009 and 85 percentage of the population are covered by Statutory Health Insurance [9]. In Nigeria, the contributions to the health insurance are calculated from 15% of the employee's basic salary, and they are divided between the employee contributing 5% and employers contributing 10% [24]. As the result, the three-dimension pooling risk framework operates to provide all of the insured population with access to needed healthcare treatment services and to protect them from out-of-pocket spending on health.

3. THE FORMULATION OF THE SIX-DIMENSION POOLING RISK FRAMEWORK

In this study, the existing three-dimension pooling risk framework was transformed to the six-dimension pooling risk framework, through the synthesis of three-dimension pooling risk framework of the health insurance scheme-Bismarck Model, with the functions of universal health insurance coverage program based on SDG 1,2,3,6, and10, the four levels of prevention, the district health system, and the district division administrative disaggregation data framework.

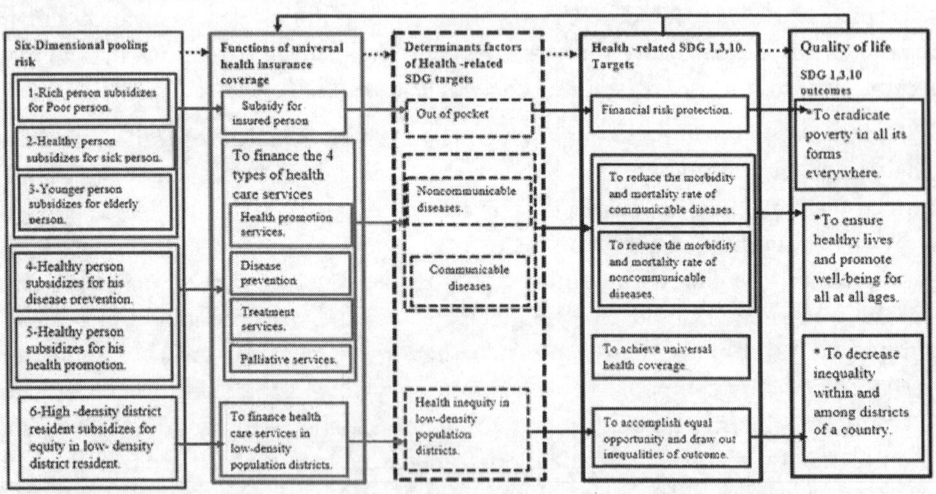

Figure3. the six-dimensional pooling risk framework

Figure 3. The six-dimension pooling risk framework.

The innovative cross-subsidization of the six-dimension pooling risk framework is composed of the rich subsidizing the poor, healthy people subsidizing sick people, the young subsidizing the elderly, the healthy people subsidizing for their health promotion, and disease prevention, and high-density-population district residence subsidizing for health equity in low-density-population districts residence (Figure 3). The innovative cross-subsidization functions to subsidize for an insured person, to finance the four types of healthcare services, and to finance healthcare services in low-density-population districts (Figure 3). Those functions address the determinant factors of health-related SDG targets, which are out of pocket, communicable diseases, noncommunicable diseases, and health inequity in low-density-population districts (Figure 3). Those functions interact with the determinant factors of health-related SDG targets financial risk protection (Figure 3).

The subsidization interacts with out of pocket schemes to offer financial risk protection for eradicating poverty in all its forms everywhere (Figure 3). Health promotion and disease prevention services transform behavioral factors, environmental factors, and epidemiological factors to reduce the morbidity and mortality rate of noncommunicable and communicable diseases (Figure 3). The reduction of morbidity and mortality rate creates healthy lives and promotes well-being for all at all ages (Figure 3). The six-dimension pooling risk framework finances healthcare services in low-density-population districts that aims to achieve health equity in low-density-population districts and to decrease inequality within and among districts of a country (Figure 3).

This study implies the guideline structure on how to implement the six-dimension pooling risk framework on a health insurance scheme. It recommends the premium equation of health insurance–Bismarck model is essential to restructure based on equity and probability of health and illness, for applying the six-dimension pooling risk framework in a health insurance scheme, to generate funds for financing the four types of healthcare services and leaving no low-density-populations districts behind. Furthermore, the guideline structure forms the premium of the framework to be between a government, employers, and employees. The framework has significant impact on economic growth, so the guidelines recommend the government to allocate resources from taxes to finance leaving no low-density-populations districts behind SDG1,2,3,6 and 10. The guidelines imply the employers need to contribute to the premium for financing community-related health promotion and disease prevention programs because the framework influences productivity. Furthermore, the framework functions to improve the quality of life of the insured population, so it is proposed the employees to contribute to the premium for financing personal-related health promotion and disease prevention programs. The package of benefits will be designated based on community and individual needs and the health-related

SDGs targets. The package of benefits will address the social and microbiological determinants of health and inequity in low-density-population districts. The health insurance scheme pays providers of health promotion and disease prevention services at the community, healthcare facilities, educational institutions, and others. In contract, the providers provide health promotion and disease prevention services to the community and the individual. Future studies are needed to transform the guideline structure formula for the premium of the framework and to formulate health promotion and disease prevention services at all levels based on the WHO, the existing theoretical frameworks, and national frameworks for accelerating the progress on the health-related SDGs targets.

4. DISCUSSION

This research compared the capability of the innovative six-dimension pooling risk framework of the health insurance-Bismarck model with the existing three-dimension pooling risk framework, in financing the theoretical frameworks for transforming the determinant factors of health-related SDGs.

The world's leading causes of death are premature deaths from noncommunicable diseases, which continue to decline [25]. The progress has slowed in current years, so urgent and targeted programs will be required for key risk factors of noncommunicable diseases, which include tobacco use and alcohol consumption, hypertension, obesity, and physical inactivity [25]. Millions of people die from communicable diseases each year even though the number of deaths has declined [25]. The deaths from communicable diseases occur in lower-resource settings where many individuals cannot access quality healthcare services [25]. We must continue to concentrate on the equitable distribution of healthcare services and provide access to quality, affordable, and effective programs in all countries and for all populations, for closing these gaps and meeting SDGs [25].

Global action plans for the prevention and control of noncommunicable diseases 2013–2020 proposed a vision, goals, voluntary global targets, and objectives [26]. The vision of Global action plan is "A world free of the avoidable burden of noncommunicable diseases" and its goal is "To reduce the preventable and avoidable burden of morbidity, mortality and disability due to noncommunicable diseases by means of multisectoral collaboration and cooperation at national, regional and global levels, so that populations reach the highest attainable standards of health and productivity at every age and those diseases are no longer a barrier to well-being or socio-economic development" [26].

The WHO and partners approached the strategic framework for ending preventable maternal mortality (EPMM) [27]. The EPMM framework composed of

SDG target 3.1: reduced global MMR to less than 70 per 100,000 live births by 2030 and five strategic objectives [27]. The five strategic objectives for EPMM include 1: To address inequities in access to quality of sexual, reproductive, maternal, and newborn health care, 2: To ensure universal health coverage for comprehensive sexual, reproductive, maternal, and newborn health care, 3: To address all causes of maternal mortality, reproductive, and maternal morbidities and related disabilities, 4: To strengthen health systems to respond to the needs and priorities of women and girls, 5: To ensure accountability to improve quality of care and equity [27].

The WHO African Region articulated the framework for provision of essential health services through strengthened district/local health systems to support UHC in the context of the SDGs [28]. The framework demonstrated the situation of universal healthcare services in the region, and the findings showed universal healthcare service coverage was 48%, universal essential healthcare service coverage was 36%, the accessibility of the population was 32%, and universal financial risk protection coverage was 34% [28]. The framework predicts that by 2030, 80% of the population will have access to essential healthcare services in 80% of Member States, and 80% of districts will have universal healthcare facility-community coverage in 80% of Member States [28].

The six-dimension pooling risk framework addresses communicable and noncommunicable diseases and inequity in low-density-population districts as determining factors of health-related SDGs for accelerating the progress. Therefore, the framework reallocates healthcare resources for communicable and noncommunicable disease healthcare services, equity in low-density-population districts, the strategic framework for ending preventable maternal mortality, global action plan for the prevention and control of noncommunicable diseases, the framework for provision of essential health services through strengthened district/local health systems of the WHO African Region. In contrast, the existing three-dimension pooling risk framework is sickness fund approach, so it is not able to remobilize healthcare resources for those frameworks.

5. LIMITATIONS

This research did not explore the impact of financing health promotion and disease prevention healthcare services on control and reduction of treatment healthcare services expenditure. In addition, this research did not figure out the impact of mobilization of healthcare resources toward low-density-populations districts on finance risk protection of poor. Future studies are needed to formulate the premium of the health insurance–Bismarck model according to probability of health and illness and equity in low-density-populations districts for implementing the framework. Finally, how to finance personal health and population health programs requires more cooperation studies between multidisciplinary public health organizations.

6. CONCLUSION

The functions of the universal health insurance coverage–Bismarck Model were formulated according to SDG 1, 2,3,6 and 10 targets after the desired outcomes of health-related SDGs and the UHC framework were synthesized. Those functions were designed to protect insured populations from financial risk, and to finance health promotion, disease prevention, treatment, and palliative health care services, and equity in low-density-population districts. The existing three-dimension pooling risk framework of the health insurance scheme-Bismarck Model was transformed to the six-dimension pooling risk framework, based on the functions of the universal health insurance coverage–Bismarck Model. The existing cross-subsidization of the three-dimension pooling risk framework is built on the rich subsidizing the poor, healthy people subsidizing sick people, and the young subsidizing the elderly. In contrast, the innovative cross-subsidization of the six-dimension pooling risk framework was created based on the rich subsidizing the poor, healthy people subsidizing sick people, the young subsidizing the elderly, the healthy people subsidizing for their own health promotion, and disease prevention, and high-density-population district subsidizing for equity in low-density-population districts. The innovative cross-subsidization of the six-dimension pooling risk framework shifts the health insurance from disease funding to human capital investment, to remobilize healthcare resources toward WHO frameworks, theoretical UHC frameworks, and national frameworks for accelerating the progress on the health-related SDGs, particularly in low-income countries, the world's least developed countries, and the Member States in the WHO African Region. The premium equation of health insurance–Bismarck model is required to restructure based on probability of health and illness, and equity in low-density-population districts, for implementing the framework in health insurance schemes.

REFERENCES

1. United Nations. Transforming our world: The 2030 agenda for sustainable development: United Nations. 2015, United Nations
2. Boerma T et al. Monitoring progress towards universal health coverage at country and global levels. PLoS Medicine. 2014;11(9):e1001731
3. World Health Organization, World health statistics 2020: monitoring health for the SDGs, Sustainable Development Goals. Geneva, Switzerland: World Health Organization; 2020

4. World Health Organization. World health statistics 2016: Monitoring health for the SDGs, Sustainable Development Goals. Geneva, Switzerland: World Health Organization; 2016

5. World Health Organization. World health statistics 2018: monitoring health for the SDGs, Sustainable Development Goals. Geneva, Switzerland: World Health Organization; 2018

6. The United Nations Statistics Division, Global indicator framework for the Sustainable Development Goals and targets of the 2030 Agenda for Sustainable Development. New York, NY: United Nations; 2017. p. 10017

7. World Health Organization, The world health report 2013: research for universal health coverage. 2013, World Health Organization: Geneva, Switzerland

8. World Health Organization. Tracking Universal Health Coverage: First Global Monitoring Report. Geneva, Switzerland: World Health Organization; 2015

9. Tulchinsky TH. Case Studies in Public Health || Bismarck and the Long Road to Universal Health Coverage. Amsterdam, Netherland: Elsevier Inc; 2018

10. Ralph J, Di Clemente LFS, Crosby RA. Health behavior theory for public health: Principles, foundation, and applications. The United States of America Jones & Bartlett Learning. 2013

11. Theodore HT, Varavikova EA. The New Public Health. 2nd ed. USA: Elsevier; 2009

12. World Health Organization. What is health promotion? Geneva, Switzerland: World Health Organization. https://www.who.int/news-room/questions-and-answers/item/health-promotion. [Cited 30 May 2022]

13. Evans TC, Evans AMR, Fidler DB, Lindelow AH, Mills M, Scheil-Adlung AX. Thailand's Universal Coverage Scheme: Achievements and Challenges. Nonthaburi, Thailand: Health Insurance System Research Office; 2012

14. Kitreerawutiwong N, Jordan S, Hughes D. Facility type and primary care performance in sub-district health promotion hospitals in Northern Thailand. PLoS One. 2017;12(3):e0174055

15. Tejativaddhana P et al. Developing primary health care in Thailand. Public Administration and Policy. 2018;21(1):36-49

16. Mansour A et al. District division administrative disaggregation data framework for monitoring leaving no one behind in the National Health Insurance Fund of Sudan: Achieving sustainable development goals in 2030. International Journal for Equity in Health. 2021;20(1):5

17. World Health Organization. The World Health Report: Health Systems Financing: The Path to Universal Coverage. Geneva, Switzerland: World Health Organization; 2010

18. Mathauer I et al. Pooling financial resources for universal health coverage: Options for reform. Bulletin of the World Health Organization. 2020;98(2):132-139

19. Mathauer I, Saksena P, Kutzin J. Pooling arrangements in health financing systems: A proposed classification. International Journal for Equity in Health. 2019;18(1):198

20. Bazyar M et al. The experiences of merging health insurance funds in South Korea, Turkey, Thailand, and Indonesia: A cross-country comparative study. International Journal for Equity in Health. 2021;20(1):66

21. Vilcu I et al. Subsidized health insurance coverage of people in the informal sector and vulnerable population groups: trends in institutional design in Asia. International Journal for Equity in Health. 2016;15(1):165

22. Orem JN, Zikusooka CM. Health financing reform in Uganda: How equitable is the proposed National Health Insurance scheme? International Journal for Equity in Health. 2010;9(1):23

23. Nsiah-Boateng E, Aikins M. Trends and characteristics of enrolment in the National Health Insurance Scheme in Ghana: A quantitative analysis of longitudinal data. Global Health Research and Policy. 2018;3(1):32

24. Mohammed S et al. Performance evaluation of a health insurance in Nigeria using optimal resource use: Health care providers perspectives. BMC Health Services Research. 2014;14(1):127

25. World Health Organization. World health statistics 2021: monitoring health for the SDGs, Sustainable Development Goals. Geneva, Switzerland: World Health Organization; 2021

26. World Health Organization, Global action plan for the prevention and control of noncommunicable diseases 2013-2020. 2013, Geneva, Switzerland: World Health Organization

27. World Health Organization. In: IGO LCBNS, editor. Trends in maternal mortality 2000 to 2017: estimates by WHO, UNICEF, UNFPA, World Bank Group and the United Nations Population Division. Geneva: World Health Organization; 2019

28. World Health Oraanization. Framework for provision of essential health services through strengthened district/local health systems to support UHC in the context of the SDGS. In: Regional Office for Africa. Brazzaville, Republic of Congo; 2019

INDEX